THE COMPLETE FORTUNE TELLER

THE COMPLETE FORTUNE TELLER

MARC LEMEZMA

GRAMERCY BOOKS
NEW YORK

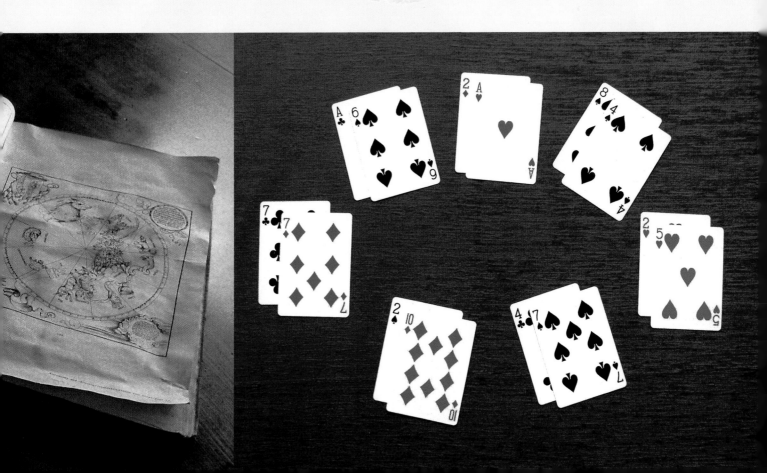

This 2007 edition is published by Gramercy Books,
an imprint of Random House Value Publishing, a division of
Random House, Inc., New York, by arrangement with
New Holland Publishers (UK) Ltd.

Gramercy is a registered trademark and the colophon is a
trademark of Random House, Inc.

Random House
New York • Toronto • London • Sydney • Auckland
www.valuebooks.com

Printed and bound in Malaysia

A catalog record for this title is available from
the Library of Congress

ISBN: 978-0-517-23050-3

1 2 3 4 5 6 7 8 9 10

CONTENTS

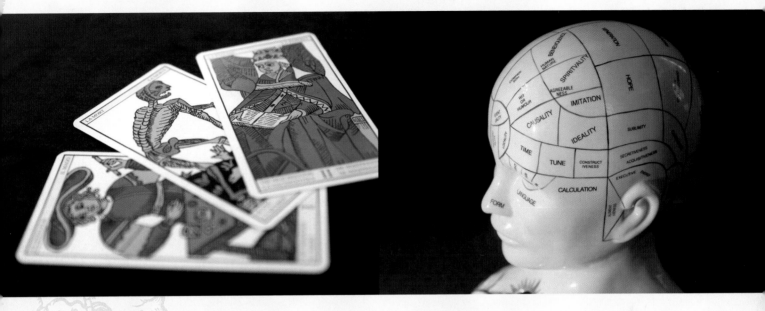

FORTUNE TELLING IN CONTEXT

Life is a journey, like any trip you or I might make on a daily basis.

We know (more or less) where we are start-ing from and where we hope to end up. This is, of course, true of our lives, as we know we are born, we exist, and then we pass away into the inde-finable realm of death.

Sadly from this point on the analogy starts to become less reliable. We do know at least an approximate route for our daily journeys: we know which roads to take and the waypoints we must pass through to get

to our chosen destination. Yet despite knowing where it will end, we never know quite where life will take us next.

This is because, while we are conscious of the beginning and end of our journeys, we only see the start of our life in retrospect and very few of us are truly aware of our impending death. So it is no surprise that mankind has constantly looked for some kind of reference to pinpoint where he "is" and a map to help direct the journey onward.

Inspiration and guidance have been sought from a hugely diverse range of sources. Some are from within the individual, others are from nature—most frequently from objects that surround our lives.

So from fire, water, the stars, and even his own body, ancient man found a thousand

ways to interpret his world, give himself some sense of context, and try to "see" what might lie ahead for him.

In the last 400 years or so, and certainly since the late 19th century, there has been a clear diver-gence in the relevance and use of mystic arts. On the one hand, certain people, such as magicians and conjurors, began to create sheer wonder and incredible theater by defying the laws of nature and science, pure-ly for the sake of enter-tainment. In parallel, the belief in fortune telling, psychics, and the like became less acceptable to the establishment but found growing favor among the masses.

In the last 50 years, the world of fortune telling has become *big* business, with psychics available 24 hours a day on premium-rate phone lines, and charging sizeable fees for personal readings. Numerous clairvoyants and mediums have become huge media stars.

I am not convinced that this is such a good thing, for what our ancestors found in their early oracles was a chance to reflect on their lives and make decisions after lengthy contem-plation. Their chosen device for seeing the future was simply a tool. Nowadays it appears that people are only too willing to let others direct their lives for them; it seems we have lost the ownership of our own destinies.

MY JOURNEY IN FORTUNE TELLING

Since I was a child, I have always felt that there has been a mystical, and sometimes spiritual, narrative running somewhere in the background of my life.

My father had strong, and perhaps uncon–ventional, spiritual beliefs, which I suspect stemmed from his deep dislike of organized religions. Having been "adopted" into a religious organization and subsequently shipped abroad as a slave farm laborer, you can perhaps understand why he may have felt this way.

He often told me stories of his "visions." I recall one such tale in which his grandmother appeared, floating in the room before him. And so, for my family and me, these oddball occurrences seemed more or less normal.

As a child I played games with family and friends that had some mystical context—perhaps palm reading or trying to see if we did indeed look like a typical example of our star sign.

My love for magic and mysticism seemed to grow with every year and, as you will see throughout this book, I have explored a great many aspects of fortune telling—sometimes in great depth, occasionally dabbling, but always with passion and deep interest.

I have always been fascinated with the plethora of fortune telling methods both in use today and also throughout history. However, one major dimension of modern "fortune telling" unsettles me immensely.

In my work as a professional magician, I have used much of the symbolism associated with prediction and divination in order to help me create an ambience that will enhance my performances. However, I would never be so bold as to claim real psychic powers to a magical audience. I might choose to leave open questions for people to work out for themselves, but I make sure that I never forget

that I am there to entertain—I have to ensure that this is my boundary.

Another side-effect of having an in-depth knowledge of the way magic tricks work is that I often see how some fake fortune tellers and psychics go about their business.

It may, for example, be as simple as the "fortune teller" repeating a basic script that appears to mean something to everyone. Sometimes it might be the use of subterfuge to gain a little knowledge about their subject and use that to build their confidence—often before spouting complete nonsense, which is then accepted on the basis of their prior deception.

Others go to great lengths to find out, in advance, what they can about those who come to see their shows or seek advice. They then lure the unsuspecting victim into their confidence by telling them some real facts—knowledge to which they would not normally have access.

I have never lost interest in the art of fortune telling and have practiced many methods, but as I grew older and wiser, I have managed to find ways to use it to my best advantage. I have learnt not to get too narrowly focused on one area and to learn that life has many lessons for us all. All we have to do is look for them and, I hope, take some notice of what they are telling us.

Thus, just like any discipline in life, the world of "fortune telling" is home to some good principles, which are often misunderstood, misused, and, quite frankly, badly abused. And so, sadly, those who have some real ability become wrongly associated with fakes and charlatans, causing their talents to be lost in the mist.

Because of this, I felt that there was a need to find a better context in which to place fortune telling, which gives it relevance, logic, and personal ownership.

CLASSES OF FORTUNE TELLING

I have worked with many methods of fortune telling over the last 35 years or so and, as a young man, I believed they all could help in every circumstance. As the years have passed I have realized that the various types and classes have specific attributes and can add value in different ways.

If you read some of the currently published literature on the subject, "fortune telling" can typically be broken down into the following groups:

Fortunes From Within the Individual
Including palmistry, biorhythms, and graphology, for example.

Fortunes From Nature
Including astrology, pyromancy (from fire), and hydromancy (from water).

Random Fortunes
Including the reading of cards, the Ancient Tarot, and rune stones.

Abstract Fortunes
Including scrying and clairvoyance, for example.

While I cannot argue with the logic of these groupings I have formed a different way of defining them:

Personal Fortunes
These help us identify things about ourselves, such as our character, our physical and mental states, and how we might act or react in given situations. This group includes such disciplines as astrology, palmistry, and biorhythms.

These, if you like, tell us something about the raw materials we have and how they can affect the events in our lives.

Speculative Fortunes

The fortunes in this category pose questions about our past, present, and future, allowing us to reflect on life and speculate on potential situations and their outcomes.

This group includes all of the disciplines that use the reading of cards, stones, dice, tea leaves, and other random objects.

Perhaps these objects can be considered tools with which we can experiment and shape our lives. We can work our raw materials in various ways in order to see what possibilities exist for us.

Focused Fortunes

These differ from the Random Fortunes in a subtle manner. Rather than finding a meaning in the order of a random layout of cards, Focused Fortunes rely on clear, directed thought or contemplation. As a result, they are great for problem solving and decision making.

This group includes such methods as scrying, clairvoyance, and pyromancy.

I see these techniques as representing inspiration—that artistic spark, which enables us to complete our picture.

I feel that this way of grouping gives you a more identifiable process for practical fortune telling. It is not just a matter of choosing one method and trying to understand everything from that one source.

Given one or more technique from each of these groups, you will be in a strong position to look at someone, understand something of who they are, speculate on what may occur, and thus consider how life may pan out for them.

Undoubtedly, there will be some people who object to the approach I have taken.

Some traditional clairvoyants and psychics may not agree with my dismissal of the very element they thrive upon—absolutes. All I ask of them is that they allow their minds (and thus the minds of their customers) to open up to more possibilities.

Some magicians working as "psychics" may object to the fact that in this and other books I have exposed their dishonesty. Sadly, there are those in my profession who have found out that they can give what appear to be meaningful "readings" by using a little knowledge and some trickery, along with a few psychological ploys. In my belief, a deception such as this has one valid purpose—entertainment. When it is used to exploit, a veil of shame shrouds the proceedings.

Certain religious factions may object, as they sometimes do, to the "demonic" practices they believe fortune tellers indulge in. I ask them to explain what could possibly be so wrong about looking into your own heart or into the eyes of Mother Nature for guidance and inspiration?

USING THIS BOOK

This leads me to the practical aspects of using this book. With so many methods of "reading fortunes" available I could not possibly even hope to mention them all.

What I do hope to do is to introduce you to a few of the more popular methods and how they work so that you can begin to practice with them yourself. These have all played a role in shaping my life—some more than others—and I offer them to you as more than simply a sampler.

In each chapter, I include a short history of each technique, along with examples of how these methods have been used in the past.

Where necessary I have provided charts, diagrams, and tables, which lay out the relevant meanings and descriptions. These are followed up with example readings for which I have used real people. You will understand that we have been discreet in not fully revealing their identities.

I also hope to provide some guidance as to the extent and limitations of the various methods. I will also tell you a little about how and where to do readings—and more importantly when not to.

There is enough here, in my belief, to enable you to give sound readings for yourself, your family and friends.

Of course, after experimenting with a few of the tools in this book, you will no doubt develop a preference for one or the other and from there you can research your favorite further in books and on the Internet.

Most importantly, I have given you a full glossary because there are numerous unusual words, phrases, and terms to get used to. The most commonly featured of these, I feel, should be explained here: "querrant"—the person for whom you are reading a fortune.

If there was one thing that I wanted to say before you begin this book, it is this:

Above all, I want to help put the simplicity and purity back into the art of "fortune telling." I want you to learn how to have fun with readings for you and your friends, but I also want to try and teach you how you can use a reading to aid serious self-reflection—the one element that is so important yet seems to be completely lost!

Marc Lemezma

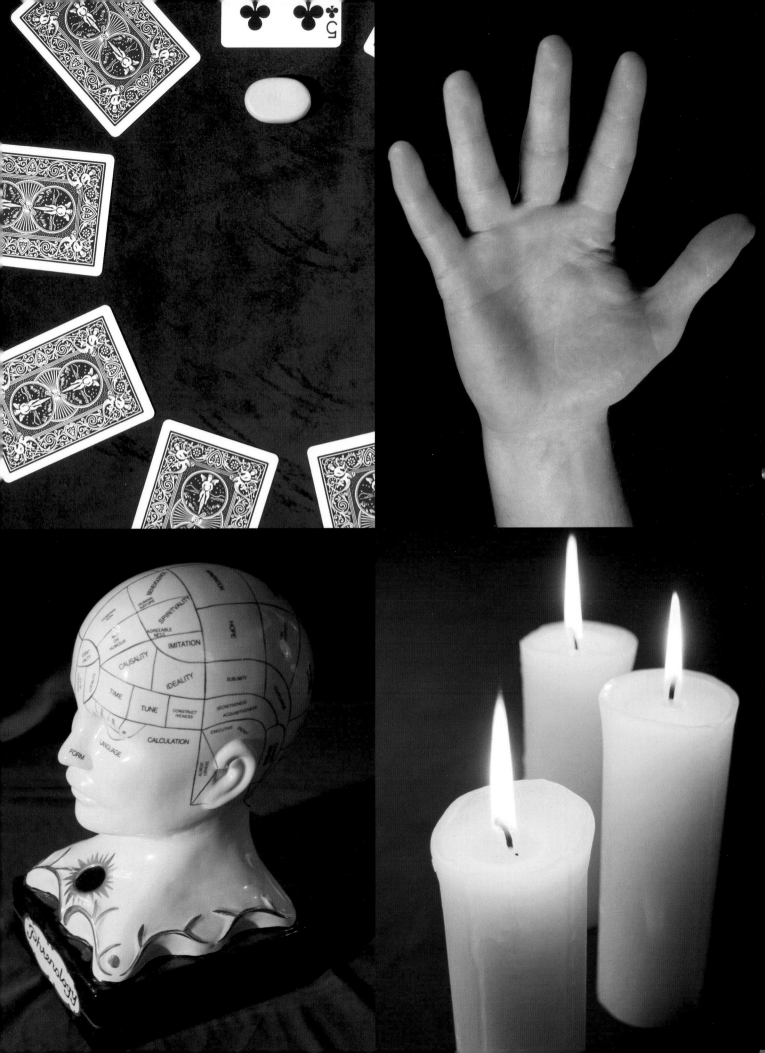

ASTROLOGY

YOUR LIFE IN THE STARS?

Did you flip through a daily newspaper to find your horoscope today? I wonder what they said and if those one hundred or so words seemed to make sense to you. If you were to do a quick survey of how your friends felt about today's horoscopes I suspect that many of them will report positively. This is because the writers often cover generalities related to our problems and challenges in life, and our aspirations and hopes. It is, perhaps, in practice, unrealistic to expect the future of one twelfth of the population to be covered accurately in a couple of paragraphs. So is there any real meaning in astrology? For me the answer has to be yes, but not when it comes to the stuff in newspapers...

Our first chapter explores the origins of astrology and offers a context to explore how our date of birth can influence our personal characteristics, some of which manifest themselves in the way we look, others in the way we behave. Just for a little fun, it will also explore how the stars affect our relationships.

THE ORIGINS & HISTORY OF ASTROLOGY

Astrology is perhaps the oldest and most widely used form of fortune telling. The zodiac we use today goes back to around 2000BC, but the roots of astrology go back to the very origins of human history. Our early ancestors did not fail to notice the cycles that occurred all around them: the light of day and the darkness of night; the changing faces of the moon; the warmth and cold of the different seasons.

They knew that the sun and the other heavenly bodies controlled the pace of life, setting the rhythm for what man had to do to survive. Thus it is no wonder that almost all cultures have attached great significance to the changing patterns in the sky.

The ancient Babylonians were among the first to create a calendar, which predicted the changing of the seasons and the movement of the sun, moon, and stars. There was a practical reason for doing this as it told them when, for example, to sow their seeds and when to reap the harvest.

They divided the sky into 12 sections, each being some 30° across. Within each section, they could see a pattern made up by the stars, which represented the animals and mythological characters that they knew. This is how the zodiac was born, along with the star signs we know today.

Astrology is an immensely complex subject requiring some significant study to enable you to draw up useable and meaningful astrological charts. Even when the work is done, while you are left with what ought to be a good analysis of your subject's characteristics, the "future" is not really there to see. We may be able to foresee suggestions of "what might be," just as we can with cards and runes, for example.

And so, for the purposes of this book, I have decided to give you a good overview of the characteristics of each sign, which can easily be detected in the character and temperament of the people around you. This, along with our interpretation of the hands, gives us a good grounding in understanding them a little better. This is the foundation of a good reading, no matter what discipline you follow.

THE STAR SIGNS & THEIR CHARACTERISTICS

We are who we are, of that there is no doubt. But what makes us that person? What forces are at work, shaping our characters? Of course our family situation, education, and culture all have an effect on us, but we must not forget that our fundamental characteristics are the starting point for all of these changes. I wonder if you can see yourself or any of your family and friends revealed by their star sign!

One of my earliest memories relating to "fortune telling" is sitting at home, leafing through a children's encyclopedia. My father used to sell them and so we were lucky enough to have a full set at home. Over the years he had instilled a sense of the spiritual and mystical in myself and all of my family.

Among the many articles that were included in the encyclopedia, there was a section on astrology, which incorporated pictures of the faces of individuals born under each star sign. It described the art of physiognomy—the correlation of a person's facial features to their star sign and its dominant characteristics.

We would spend hours comparing the faces in the book with our own and those of our friends and family. Cheekily, we even tried to work out the star signs of our school teachers, based upon our childish misinterpretations of their characters.

Whilst my siblings and I do bear quite a strong family resemblance, we were able to spot the nuances in each other's faces and the character traits associated with our given sign. Despite the interesting results we achieved, I have often wondered if we were just simply seeing what we wanted to see.

Perhaps I should give you the opportunity to make your own mind up. Thus, to begin with, here is a breakdown of each sign's associated symbol, element, and ruling planet, along with typical personality traits.

Aries, Ram, Fire, Mars
(March 21–April 19)

If you ever hear the words, "Watch out, I'm coming through!," you might just see an Arian on a mission. Arians tend to be quite independent and driven: their competitive nature can make them overwhelmingly arrogant and domineering. Sometimes their drive makes them a little too hasty for their own good!

Taurus, Bull, Earth, Venus
(April 20–May 20)

Taureans are typically dependable and patient: they are indeed "as solid as a rock." Their stoic attitude allows them to plod along happily—perhaps too happily, as they are often stubborn and immovable. Sometimes they can be selfish and overpossessive, especially when it comes to their emotions. This can quite often lead to them suddenly lashing out in anger. I wouldn't want to be around when that happens!

Gemini, Twins, Air, Mercury
(May 21–June 20)

Geminis are very expressive, creative, and inquisitive. This makes them very flexible in life: they mix well with all kinds of people, and quite literally "go with the flow." On the other hand, they can be a little restless, which may lead them into scheming behind other people's backs. Their lack of focus and direction, however, will often lead them to slip up.

Cancer, Crab, Water, Moon
(June 21–July 22)

People born under Cancer are often the kind of friend we wish we didn't have. They are like "the teenager who never grew up." They are sensitive and caring on the one hand, yet, on the other, they can be extremely lazy. Their selfishness can make them try to get their way at all costs and also get out of doing what must be done when they don't want to.

Leo, Lion, Fire, Sun
(July 23–August 22)

I am a Leo, and to be quite honest I am a very typical example! I am creative and like to perform. I know that "the show must go on." Sometimes I can be a little pretentious and I always like to get my own way. I am very proud of what I, myself, and my family, have done, often to the point of being overbearing.

Virgo, Virgin, Earth, Mercury
(August 23–September 22)

Virgos can be quite skeptical. This is because they are very studious and thorough and like to know everything about everything. They will always be asking questions and like to "dot the Is and cross the Ts." In fact, they can be quite annoyingly thorough, to the point where they prevent things actually getting done.

Libra, Scales, Air, Venus
(September 23–October 22)

Librans are represented by the scales for a reason: they crave to be "all things to all men." They like to be perfectly balanced and show no favoritism. They can make great diplomats, because they have the knack of telling everybody just what they want to hear. Sometimes this desire for equality backfires, however, making them appear indecisive and even hypocritical.

Scorpio, Scorpion, Water, Mars/Pluto
(October 23–November 21)

Scorpios seem to know what to do in any situation. They have a great natural resourcefulness that makes them great parents and carers. They truly do have a "sting in the tail," though, for they can be very temperamental. Be careful never to upset a Scorpio, because they can be extremely vicious and vindictive when crossed.

Sagittarius, Archer, Fire, Jupiter (November 22–December 21)

Sagittarians are warm and generous. They can be quite deep thinkers, who take time to consider the implications of what goes on around them. Because of the time they spend thinking, they usually believe they are right! And so, they can sometimes come across as quite arrogant and blunt.

Capricorn, Goat, Earth, Saturn (December 22–January 19)

Capricorns often suffer with "blind ambition." They are hard working and as honest as the day is long, but there is a price to pay, for they seem to ignore those who are in their way or who are not involved in their plan. As a result, they can sometimes seem cold, unemotional, and unrelenting.

Aquarius, Water–bearer, Air, Saturn/Uranus (January 20–18 February)

Aquarians are truly "rebels with a cause." They are independent, free thinkers, who seem to want the best for everyone. They often go about things in unusual or unorthodox ways, and are willing to pioneer new ideas and concepts. However, they may not be loyal and can be very unpredictable.

Pisces, Fish, Water, Jupiter/Neptune (February 19–March 20)

"You're nothing but a dreamer" is a good way to describe a typical Piscean. They are very artistic and tend to have their heads way up in the clouds. They are extremely caring and compassionate, and like to help. Sadly, though, their good intentions are often spoiled by their impractical and idealistic nature.

PHYSIOGNOMIC READINGS

Let's face it, the way we hold our bodies and the look on our faces tells a new acquaintance volumes about who we are. But does our birth date affect the shape of our face, and therefore another's perception of our character? I was not entirely sure that it did and I initially included this section as a bit of fun. What astounded me was the remarkable results it yielded.

Physiognomy has been studied for millennia and is not always associated with astrology. It has often been supported by criminologists to identify those likely to commit crimes but, sadly, it has all too often been abused by racists, who use it to "prove" their misguided theories about people from other cultures.

When we meet someone for the first time, we make subconscious judgments about them. Much of this is based on their demeanor and dress, but a significant element of how we feel about them is determined by our interpretation of their face. Perhaps they remind us of a person we have known previously, or of a character from a book or film, or maybe their features show characteristics typical of certain star signs.

Remembering the games I played as a child, and just for a little fun, I decided to do some facial analysis in a semiscientific way. I sent Duncan, my photographer, off to collect some pictures of faces, asking him to make sure that at least some of them were people I did not know. I wanted to see whether they did truly show the facial characteristics that a physiognomist would attribute to their star sign, and I wanted there to be no preconceptions on my part about any of the individuals.

I had one challenge in this task. The books and information I had on the subject were all quite old and from a time when our society was considerably less diverse. To my surprise it produced some interesting results!

Aries

Joan's face does have the notable characteristics of her sign. The long, high sweeping eyebrows, which curve up at the outer edges are said to mimic the Ram's horns. Also, the shape of Joan's mouth is typical, with an upper lip that is longer than the lower.

Taurus

Although Gareth has his hair cut short, we can see it is thick and has a natural curl, just like a typical Taurean. He also has the wide brows and symmetrical staring eyes that are so typical of this sign.

Gemini

Geminis are said to have two distinct sides to their character and this is reflected in their facial features. As you can see Gray's face has two distinct sides, one being much lower set than the other. This can be seen clearly in his eyes and, to some extent, in the shape of his mouth. His nose and his chin point in different directions, which is very typical of a Gemini.

Cancer

Cancerians make a huge impact wherever they go—usually with very little effort! I am sure Cecilia does so too with her striking features. Here we have a typical Cancer face structure: a wide space between the eyebrows and deep eyes. Also note the high forehead with a deep curve forming the temples. However, with such thick hair, I wonder if Cecilia might be on the cusp of Leo?

Leo

Marion is a Leo. A bushy mane, thick eyebrows, slightly raised cheeks, and distinct jowls are the signs of a true Leo. Need I say more? Perhaps just this: I am a Leo (I think a truly typical Leo!) so see if you can spot those same characteristics in pictures of me elsewhere in this book.

Virgo

Take a look at Gülen's eyes and you will see they are slightly asymmetrical. Yet the rest of her face is fairly symmetrical, unlike a Gemini. Her long, elegant nose, the accentuated ridge in her upper lip, and her full cheeks, are all other characteristics typical of a Virgo.

Libra

I want you to pay attention to Steffi's chin—it is both distinct and quite V-shaped. Note also how the lines from her chin radiate nicely across her face to form dimples. This is very typical of a Libran, along with those lovely warm eyes.

Scorpio

Scorpios seem to know what to do in order to survive and stay focused. This trait shows up in their facial features quite strongly. Note Kate's wide yet focused eyes and her direct look that seems to follow you around the room. Another feature of Kate's face that is typical of Scorpio is her large flat cheeks.

Sagittarius

I had a choice of four subjects in this sign. All of them had typical Sagittarian characteristics—in particular a nose with a very distinct ball on the end. Here Hema also shows the wide smile and larger forehead, which are also common features of this sign.

Capricorn

Like the goat whose name they bear, Capricorns are usually determined. Sometimes their features reflect this with a slightly sullen look. Catherine's natural beauty belies her otherwise typical Capricorn traits. Note the prominent brow overshadowing the deep-set eyes and the quite narrow upper lip.

Aquarius

Have a close look at Adam's eyelids. They are quite small but can you see that they tilt slightly? This is a typical Aquarian trait, along with the large, square-shaped forehead and the broad tip of the nose.

Pisces

When I first saw Andrew's picture I was unsure if he had a typical Piscean face, because he was wearing thick glasses. From this shot, Andrew's well-defined eyelids and broad nose are the main clues, but the other typically Piscean facet of his face is that it shows less symmetry than some other signs.

ASTROLOGICAL LOVE MATCHES

For centuries, some people have used a person's star sign as a key factor in determining their ideal choice of a life partner. Given the varying character types of each sign, it is easy to see why there might be both good and bad combinations.

The term "Love Matches" may be considered a misnomer, because, frankly, we could fall in love with anyone—no matter what their sign is. The real issue, however, is about how that relationship functions.

Here are some thoughts on which of the various signs make good matches and which make dangerous combinations.

Aries
(March 21–April 19)

The highly driven nature of Arians means that they can be hard to build good relationships with. Other highly driven signs, such as Leo or Saggitarius, can follow along and make good life partners, although there will be plenty of action and conflict.

Slow and methodical people, such as Virgos or Taureans, will get left behind very quickly. If you really want fireworks, then put two Arians together!

Taurus
(April 20–May 20)

Good old Taurus is a solid and dependable character and therefore makes a good partner for pretty much anyone. The trouble is, though, that they can be irritated by the impetuous nature of the Fire signs. When angered, Taureans stand their ground and the conflict will deepen.

Capricorns and Pisceans make excellent partners for Taurus, perhaps only topped by a pair of Taureans together. And, if you are Sagittarian, don't even think about it!

Gemini
(May 21–June 20)

Geminis make good all–around partners for most star signs because they are so easy going and quite dependable. They are an almost perfect match for Librans, while together they can form really long–lasting relationships.

However, put a Gemini with a Taurean or, worse, with a Scorpio and you will see some interesting twists and turns in the relationship.

Cancer
(June 21–July 22)

A relaxed Cancerian is an emotional time bomb waiting to explode. Put them with a Leo or a Scorpio and that hidden passion will come to the surface very quickly. Geminis worry Cancerians because of their inquisitiveness—perhaps they are scared they will be found out.

Put two Cancerians together for plenty of love, but no action.

Leo
(July 23–August 22)

Everybody loves a Leo! Their natural exuberance and fun nature makes a Leo attractive to almost anyone, with the possible exception of Virgos—probably because they can see through a Leo's thin façade.

Put them with Arian or Sagittarian for real passion, and together for a nonstop party!

Virgo
(August 23–September 22)

Virgos are extremely pragmatic and get along well with their fellow Earth signs. Air signs will tend to irritate a Virgo so, whilst they may start well, there may be trouble ahead.

Virgos need to be reenergized from time to time and that makes them a great match for the Fire signs except, perhaps, for poor old Leo.

A perfect match, perhaps one of the best overall, is a Virgo and a Capricorn.

Libra
(September 23–October 22)

Deeply loving, Librans get on well with Geminis and Aquarians. Initially, there may be deep love between Librans and Pisceans, or Librans and Cancerians. However, these two other signs don't find it easy to talk about their feelings and emotions, which may lead to difficulties along the line.

An Arian, on the other hand, is a great match for a Libran.

Scorpio
(October 23–November 21)

Perhaps the most emotionally intense of all the signs, Scorpio relates well to Cancer and Pisces. Often Scorpios have a secret agenda that displays itself as a swift sting from their tail. This conflicts directly with Gemini's double-sided nature and is a difficult combination.

Scorpios can have great fun with the Fire signs but should be careful with Leos—they will want it all or not at all.

Sagittarius
(November 22–December 21)

Passionate and optimistic, Sagittarians can run with the Fire signs and feel the emotions of the Water signs, so these are generally good combinations. Those with solid Earth signs, such as Taureans, are less compatible, seeing Sagittarians as fanciful dreamers.

Aquarians and Arians are great with Sagittarians but, for a steamy affair, they can do no better than a Leo partner.

Capricorn
(December 22–January 19)

Poor old Capricorns often can't see the wood for the trees. They will work hard at any relationship but will often be led down a path they would rather not travel by the Fire signs. It will be good for a while, but a mistake in the long run.

They can also fall foul of a scheming Gemini or Scorpio partner. Good matches for Capricorn, on the other hand, are Taureans, Pisceans, or other Capricorns.

Aquarius
(January 20–18 February)

Articulate and open, Aquarians are great at sharing their feelings and thus get along well with the other Air signs—Librans, in particular. The ability to communicate well means that problems are resolved and the relationship seems always to be fresh.

Cancerians will often feel under pressure from an Aquarian partner—this could be the undoing of the relationship!

Pisces
(February 19–March 20)

With their deep emotional need, Pisceans tend to relate well to the other Water signs, and so relationships with Cancerians and Scorpios, in particular, will tend to be long and meaningful. Fiery Leos may be good for a fling, but their lack of depth will soon leave the relationship floundering.

For real earthy stability, however, a Capricorn makes a wise choice.

Using Astrology

As I mentioned earlier, there is not enough space in a book such as this to even begin to cover full astrological readings.

However, what you do have here is some useful groundwork on the characters of the various signs and how they might function in a relationship. These factors are all important in considering how they will react to the other readings you might give them.

THE ORIGINS OF THE ZODIAC

The actual origins of the signs that we use today are not fully understood, but I have read one theory, in a number of variations, that I feel is worthy of discussion.

We know that the Ancient Babylonians were among the first to detail the movements of the heavenly bodies. The Ancient Egyptians used the movements of stars in the sky as a form of calendar. These stars would be very familiar to them, because they frequently worked in the evening and at night, it being too hot to work through the whole day.

So how did they manage to "see" the various animals in the star formations, or constellations?

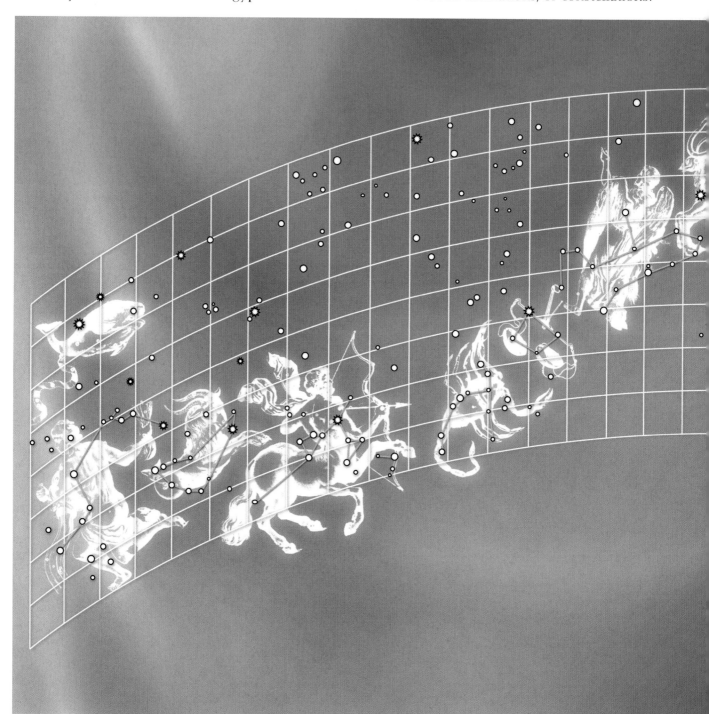

They knew, for example, that their cattle would be ready to mate each year when the sun was in a certain point of the zodiac. Thus they imag-ined a "bull" in the stars and Taurus was born!

Using the same idea they could work out when the rainy season would occur (Aquarius) and when to harvest fish (Pisces) and so on.

Having said all the above, we must remember that our ancestors in all cultures saw their lives clearly in partnership with the forces of nature and animals.

Finally, and perhaps unsurprisingly, the origin of the word zodiac is Greek, meaning "circle of animals."

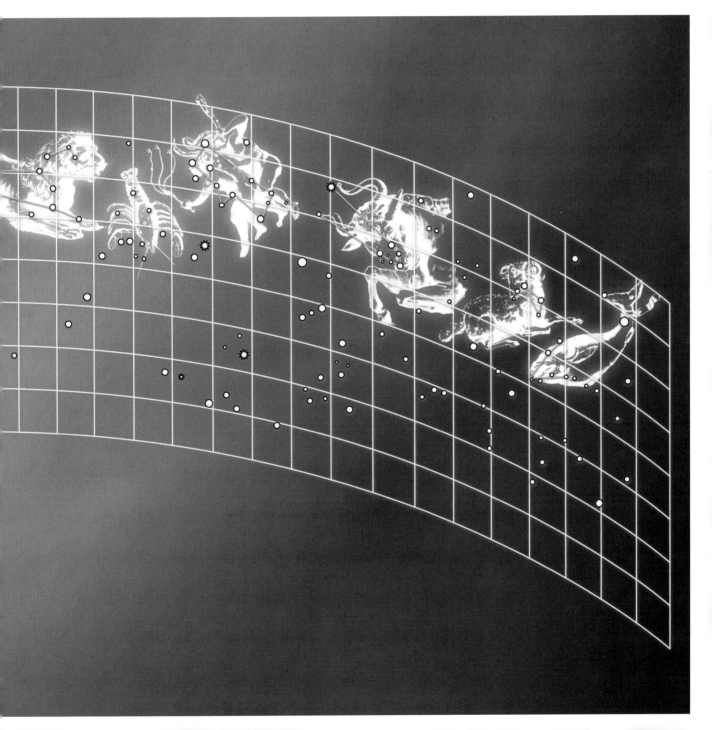

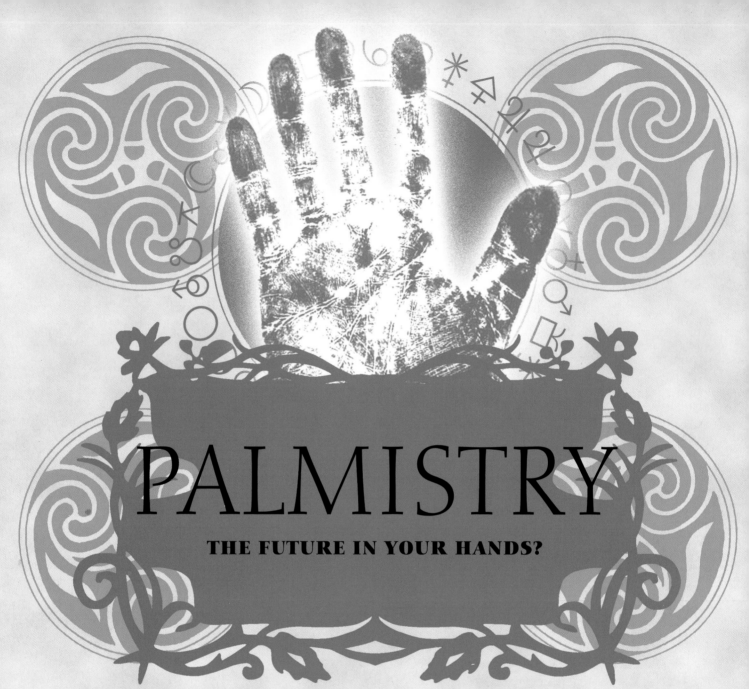

PALMISTRY

THE FUTURE IN YOUR HANDS?

Take a good, long look at your hands. Examine them front and back, notice the
shapes and lines, and how they form wondrously intricate patterns. Perhaps you
have a blemish or even a scar on one of them; I wonder what memories they
evoke. Now compare both hands: you will see subtle differences in the
lines and perhaps the signs of wear and tear on one or the other.
Humans do virtually everything with their hands, so it is no wonder that they show
a record of what we have done and how we have lived. But can our hands help us to
predict the future? Perhaps not directly in detail, but obviously the shape of any part
of our body is the result of our genetic makeup: thus it makes sense that we can
gain some understanding of our nature and the ways in which we are likely to
behave by observing their shape, size, and other details, such as lines and mounts.
This chapter also introduces the history and background of palmistry. I wonder
what your hands tell others about you!

NATURE VERSUS NURTURE

To me, the term "palmistry" is something of a misnomer, for one is interested in more than the simple lines on the palm. We need to consider the shape and size of the hand and all its component parts in order to get a whole view. Thus for me a more appropriate term would be "chirognomy" from the Greek word for hand.

There is, of course, a logic to using palm reading. Our hands start out as an indicator of what we have been given at the outset of life, not by fate or destiny so much, but simply as a result of our genetic makeup.

As we progress through life, our hands change as we use and abuse them, reflecting the impact of our everyday lives on our destiny.

The fascination with the hand and indeed its shape, structure, and detail goes back many thousands of years. It is known that the palm was used for "readings" by most of the pre-Christian civilisations, including the Greeks, Egyptians, Chinese, and Assyrians.

The ancient Chinese recognized the uniqueness of the hand to the individual so much that they used a thumbprint as a seal of authenticity. Julius Caesar was known to have chosen his generals only after reading their palm prints.

I remember going to a seaside amusement arcade as a child and dropping a penny into a machine that "read" my palm by placing it on a surface covered with moving nodules that supposedly measured the lines and indents of my hand. An automaton of a gypsy fortune teller then rattled for a few moments, then a small card popped out of a slot telling me to "Expect the unexpected!"

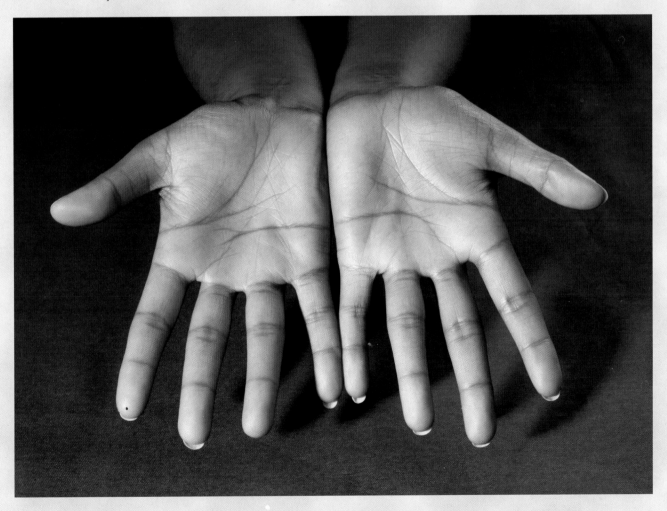

GIVING YOUR OWN PALM READINGS

Most people assume that a palm reading can be done very quickly, simply by looking at the three dominant lines—the Life Line, the Head Line, and the Heart Line. There is nothing essentially wrong in doing this, although it simply does not give the whole picture— there are a range of other elements to take into consideration.

One question I am often asked about the reading of palms is "Which hand should I use?" Well, the answer is actually both—each hand has relevance and often comparing the two can be very useful.

Typically, your dominant hand (this is most commonly the right) tells us something of your personality, talents, health, and potential, as well as how others see you. The passive hand (usually the left) contains information about your potential, your instincts, and so on. Again, there is a certain logic to this, with the left (passive) hand showing what you were born with and the right (dominant) hand showing how life has affected and changed you.

So the real question is not "which hand?" but whether you plan to do a single- or double-hand reading. For this book we will concentrate on our querrants' dominant hands.

There is so much detail that can be read, interpreted, and cross-referenced in a hand. This can sometimes mean that readings take quite a considerable time if they are being done properly—your querrant may have to sit or stand with their hand in an awkward position for half an hour or so.

Traditionally, palm readers overcame this by taking an impression of the hand and letting their querrant relax or even go elsewhere while they drew up a detailed reading.

This would have been done by applying ink to the hand with a roller and then having the querrant place their palm on a sheet of paper, leaving an image for you to work with.

There are two or three disadvantages with this approach. Firstly the image is reversed from real life, making interpretation a little more challenging, especially for the beginner. Then there is the matter of the detail that can be seen for the various "mount" regions on the palm. A simple impression makes it hard to distinguish between a large flat "mount" and, for example, a querrant who has simply pressed a little harder on the paper.

But, of course, the most obvious problem with this method is that it is inherently messy! Even with washable inks there is always a risk of staining clothes and furniture.

I am pleased to say that modern technology gives us a much neater solution in the shape of photocopiers and scanners. These can give a very detailed image of the hand, and the undulations of the "mounts" are far easier to detect. And, if you have scanned the hand into a computer, you can zoom in to areas of interest for a really close look.

If you decide to take this approach, you must be very careful not to damage the machine you use in any way. In particular, you must be careful to keep the platen glass spotlessly clean. Otherwise those who use the photocopier after you may find an image of your hand on their paperwork!

The best way to do this is to use some overhead transparency film or perhaps a clear laminating pouch, which you can lay onto the platen glass to prevent marking it.

Begin by looking at your querrant's hands. Make some written or mental notes about anything that immediately jumps out at you, so you can come back to it after you have scanned or taken an imprint from their hand.

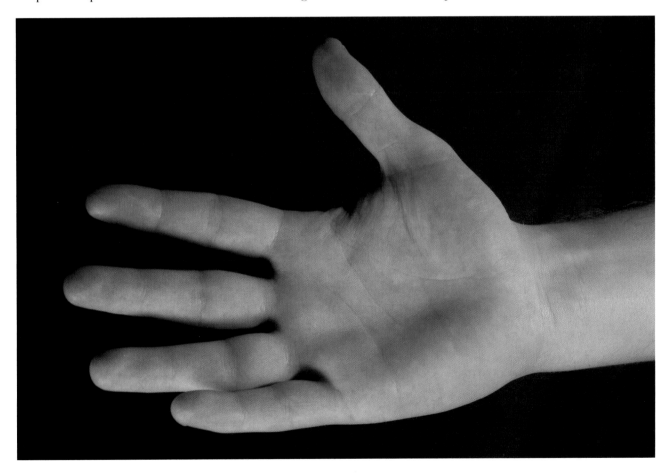

INTERPRETING THE HAND

Here we will examine three main elements of the hand: the shape, the "mounts," and the major lines. As a good starting point you might want to look at your own hand and see how the following meanings relate to yourself.

There is really so much to see in the hand that I couldn't possible cover it all in enough detail in this book. Modern palm readers have revised the traditional seven basic hand classifications into a much more manageable, and perhaps meaningful, four:

THE BASIC HAND TYPES

The Earth Hand (A):
Square palm and short fingers
If your hand is like this, you are likely to be a practical, dependable type of person, and someone who is likely to be very creative and energetic.

The Air Hand (B):
Square palm and long fingers
If your hand is like this, you may be clever and artistic, very rational, and perhaps a little overly regimented in your general approach to life.

The Fire Hand (C):
Long palm and short fingers
If your hand is like this, you could be energetic to the point of being annoyingly restless. Very individualistic, you like to live life at top speed.

The Water Hand (D):
Long palm and long fingers
If your hand is like this, you might tend to be emotional and caring; you are also likely to be one who is aware of Mother Nature and the environment.

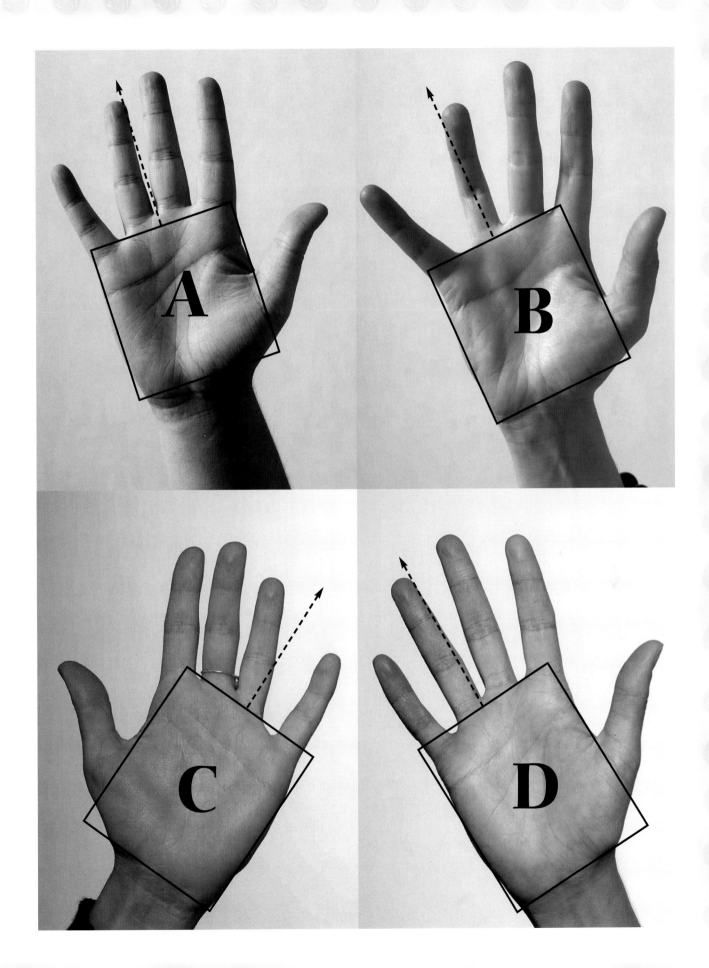

THE MOUNTS

Take a look at the palm of your hand and run your fingers gently over and across it. You will feel the gentle undulations of what are known as the "mounts." These fleshy regions tell us something about our many characteristics. The simple way to interpret them is that the larger and more well defined they are, the stronger that particular characteristic is.

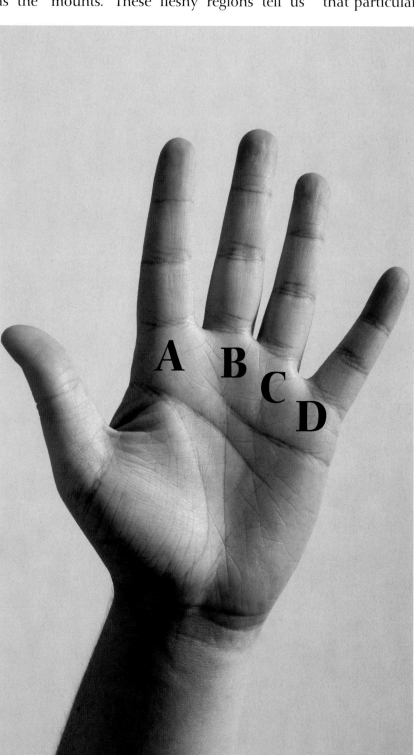

The Mount Of Jupiter (A)
This represents enthusiasm, self-worth, and ambition. A small mount here may indicate laziness or even selfishness. People with a large mount tend to be overpowering and overambitious.

Mount Of Saturn (B)
This represents sense and responsibility. A small mount here might imply a dull person with little to offer, or someone who might be a tad reckless. A large mount shows that the person might tend to be introspective and have a predisposition toward depression.

Mount Of Apollo (C)
This represents art and creativity. A small mount here may indicate that a person is short of artistic ability or direction, or perhaps suffering from a lack of finesse. A large mount, on the other hand, might indicate a rather gaudy, flamboyant individual, or someone who tends to be tacky and pretentious.

Mount Of Mercury (D)
This represents intelligence and your influence on others. A small mount indicates that you might be easily led and quiet amongst others. A large mount indicates a good sense of humor and persuasiveness— a good salesman, perhaps— erring toward misuse of your ability if it is very large.

Across the middle of the palm we find the Mounts and Planes of Mars, and this area represents emotional and moral integrity.

While one can study these three areas individually, it is more interesting to analyze them as a whole. They can be most revealing, because they give us an indication of how well balanced the attitudes of our querrant are.

Mount Of Mars
Aggressive (E)
Also known as "Mars Positive," this area indicates fighting spirit: your desire to work hard or to defend your territory, for example. An underdeveloped mount here can show that you might be weak in an argument and interested in protecting yourself rather than fighting for others. A large mount can show someone who is determined, divisive, and even sometimes cruel and manipulative.

Plane Of Mars (F)
You may have ideas but do you have the ability to turn them into reality? A large, strong, well defined Plane of Mars indicates entrepreneurial spirit. If you have difficulty telling where it begins and where the Mounts of Mars end, you may be someone who is liable to let emotions, either good or bad, get in the way of your business ventures.

Mount Of Mars
Defensive (G)
Sometimes called "Mars Negative," this shows our patient, under-standing side and the part of us that is willing to endure periods of pain to achieve a long-term goal. A well-developed mount indicates that you are more willing to accept others as they are and willing to spend time helping and nurturing. If you are one who does not suffer fools gladly, you may find you have an underdeveloped area here.

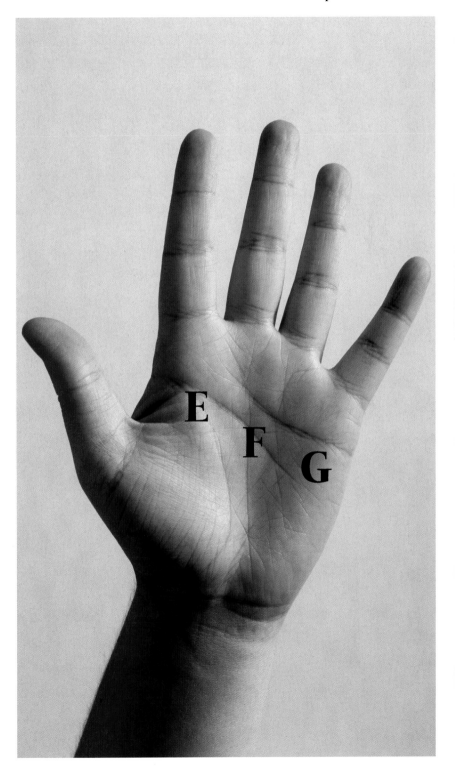

Across the lower part of the hand we have the Mounts of Venus, Neptune, and The Moon (sometimes referred to as the Mount of Luna). Whilst the Mounts and Plane of Mars deal with our morals and our general emotions, this area is more about emotional intelligence and how we see and relate to others around us, as well as to our own inner self.

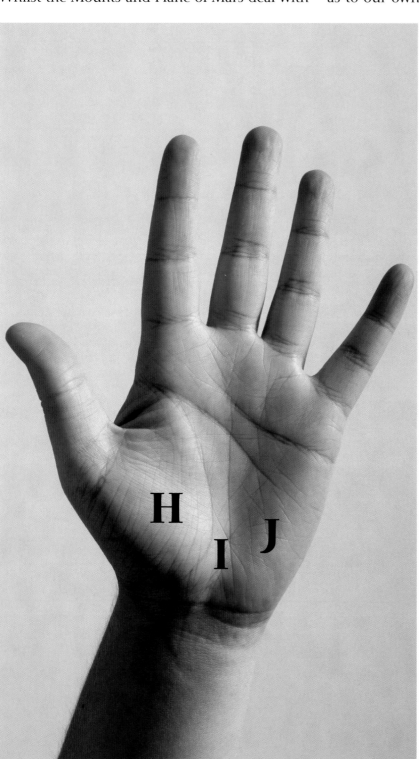

Mount Of Venus (H)

This represents your general happiness and your overall health. A small mount shows that you may have a tendency to let illness or other barriers get you down easily and prevent you from doing what needs to be done. A large mount shows that you may be the kind of person who can keep smiling through adversity, even to the point of not caring properly for your own health.

Mount Of Neptune (I)

This represents your general level of perception. A small mount could indicate that you are not particularly observant or well tuned in to the events that are going on around you. Conversely, a large mount might imply that you are unusually perceptive—perhaps even to the point of seeing things that are not even really there.

Mount Of The Moon (J)

This represents perceptiveness in romantic relationships and connections with other people. It also represents how good you are at communicating with yourself. A small mount may mean that you have a tendency to be, or appear, cold and unfeeling. A larger mount can show that you are extremely passionate and tactile in your personal relationships.

THE PRIMARY LINES

As a general rule of thumb, well–defined and clear lines indicate strength and clarity, whereas broken or weak lines tend to show interruptions or uncertainty.

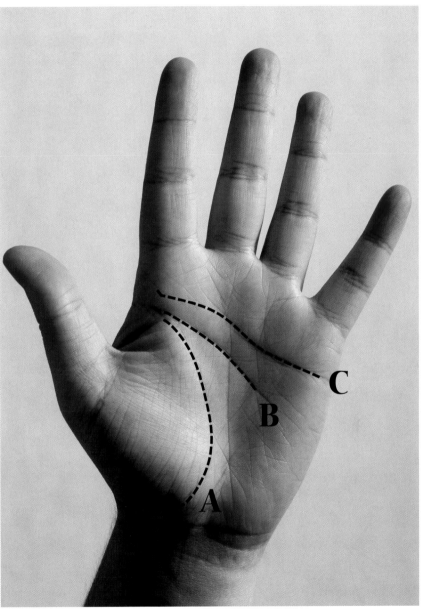

The Life Line (A)

This is not, as many believe, an indicator of your potential longevity. The Life Line is more a symbol of the way in which you might lead your life and overcome challenges.

A long and clear line indicates a positive and energetic lifestyle, while a weak line may show you prefer to be on your own—perhaps you are not a team player.

Breaks or changes of texture that are present in the line might imply that there are likely to be many changes in direction during your life. If it has lots of branches it can indicate wealth and great success.

The Head Line (B)

This represents intelligence and the inherent potential within you. This is also about how you see the world and how events shape your thinking.

A strong line carries implica–tions of great intelligence and, more importantly, an ability to focus and concentrate on getting things done. A break in the line can indicate a change of mental state in relation to something that has occurred in your life.

Many breaks or branches show that your views are likely to swing wildly as you go through the trials and tribulations that life some-times throws at you.

The Heart Line (C)

This represents your emotions and the way in which you handle relationships. A strong, clear line may imply that you let your heart rule your head, particularly if it is much longer than the Head Line.

If the line is very long and very deep and located in the upper part of the palm near the base of the fingers, you may be someone who has a tendency to be very possessive when you are in love.

If the line is weak or blurred then it may show you have difficulty in forming or sustaining relationships—perhaps you find it hard to connect deeply with others.

THE SECONDARY LINES

Almost every hand I have ever looked at has had an easily identifiable Heart, Head, and Life Line. Secondary lines, however, can sometimes be difficult or impossible to spot. Do not panic if you are missing one or two of them. It does not mean you are lacking in some area or other, it simply means that another attribute, represented by another line, is more dominant or important.

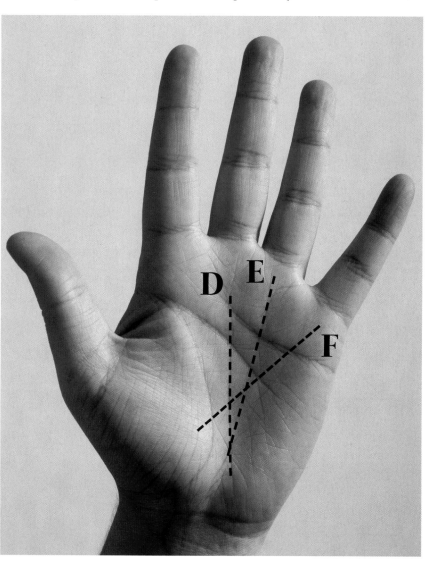

The Sun Line (E)

So what have you achieved today, and indeed throughout your life?

Far too many of us show a tendency to underplay our successes in life, because, all too often, we are likely to see them in comparison with the rich and famous celebrities in the media. However, all of us have things to be proud in our lives, that we don't recognize—albeit some more than others. We pass exams, get jobs, raise families, and beat illnesses; we all achieve.

The Sun Line sums up our actions and achievements in life. And so, when you are feeling downhearted and unsure as to what you have achieved, take a look at your Sun Line for a little inspiration.

The Mercury Line (F)

This line is concerned with your ability to focus and remain sharp and alert.

And so, a well-defined, unbroken Mercury Line might indicate a person who is a good businessman, or someone who may be regarded as a eloquent speaker or performer—certainly someone who is sharp, on the ball and witty with words. It can also be a good indication that a person likes adventure and is willing to explore, as they are unlikely to be easily deterred.

If the line is less clear and perhaps broken, this might indicate difficulty or lack of focus, and someone who might not stay the course over the long term.

The Saturn Line (D)

Sometimes known as the Fate Line, this is, for me, the least meaningful line, because it tends not to deal with potential as the others do. Instead, it implies some absolute outcomes of a person's wealth, health, and happiness, which may be unattainable. I like to think of it as an "if only" line—a line you should hopefully never look at. For, if we are to make the most of our lives, we should never look back at the past and think of what could have been.

READINGS FROM THE PALM

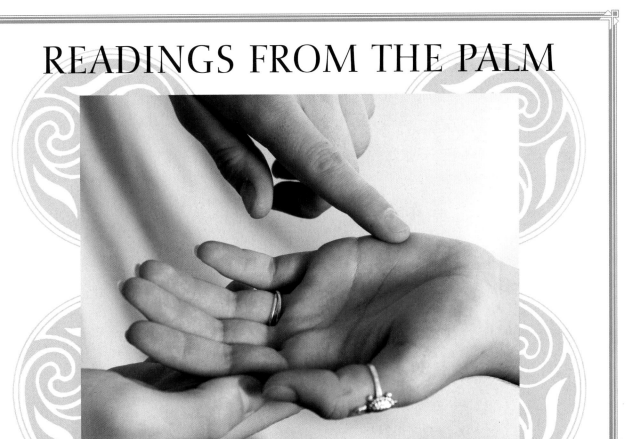

Fortune telling is something of art. While many people tend to be dismissive of the concept, I think that every one of us has a deep inner desire to "know." And, once you have got people interested, often there can be absolutely no stopping them.

Earlier in the book I took a look at some of the people from my publisher's offices and made some strong correlations between their faces and their star signs. This I think got their interest fired up because they wanted to know more, and so they set me a new challenge. They decided to test the concept of palm readings by giving me some "anonymous" hands to read.

They sent me some pictures of their own hands and those of their colleagues. I had no idea to whom the various palms belonged. I selected a handful of the more interesting ones to analyze in a little depth...

Having photographs to look at, as opposed to an actual hand, was very useful, because it gave me two distinct advantages in giving a reading. Using my computer, I was able to bring out the definition of the lines and mounts very clearly and make some useful assessments. Additionally, doing the readings in this way gave me more time to consider and think about the readings, so I could properly balance the meanings of the various elements of their hands. The most important piece of advice I can give as you give your own palm readings is to consider the hand as a whole.

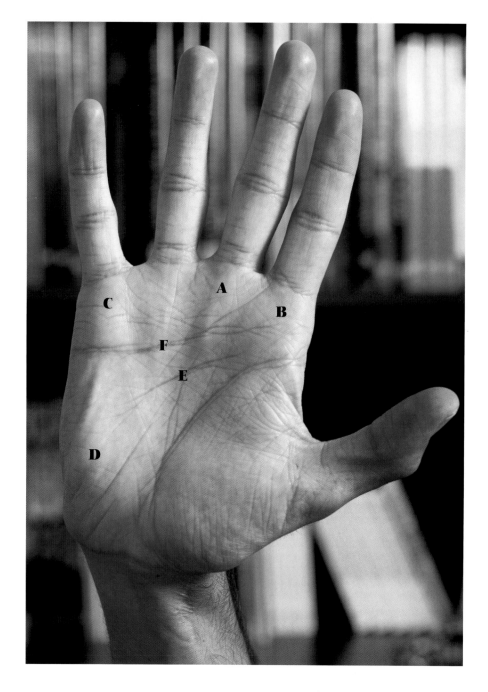

Hand I

The owner of this hand is a very creative individual. This is evident not just because of the "Air" shape but because of the configuration of the mounts. In fact I would go as far as to say that this person is happy to let go of ambition in favor of artistic achievement.

The Mounts of Saturn (A) and Jupiter (B) are quite small when compared to Mercury (C), which seems to extend and become one with the Mount of The Moon (D)—this is clearly an expressive, imaginative, and artistic soul.

There is another indication of this in their Head Line (E), which seems to be very indistinct, save for a clear section in the middle: this shows a degree of focus in one aspect of their life. The clear Heart Line (F) shows us that they are good in long-term relationships. However, the line fades and splits at one end—do they find it hard to make new relationships?

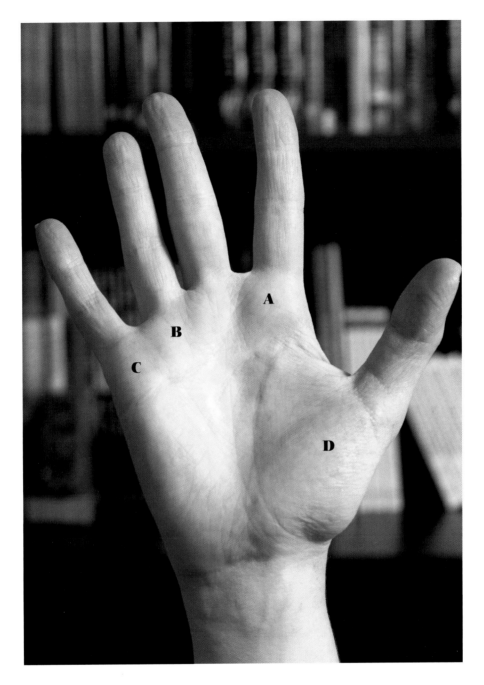

Hand II

The first thing that strikes me about this hand is the very large Mount of Jupiter (A): this represents ambition, drive, and self confidence.

Sometimes people with such a large Mount of Jupiter can be overbearing and way too pushy. However, I don't feel it is the case with this individual—their strong ambition is tempered by two other aspects in their hand.

Firstly the Mounts of Apollo (B) and Mercury (C) tell us they have the ability to create and communicate, which will always calm the negative aspects of a driven person. More importantly, the large Mount of Venus (D) indicates a very happy, healthy person.

In summary, this person has clear ambition but not "blind ambition." They are aware of other people and their needs, and they regard themselves as working hard not for their own benefit but for the greater good.

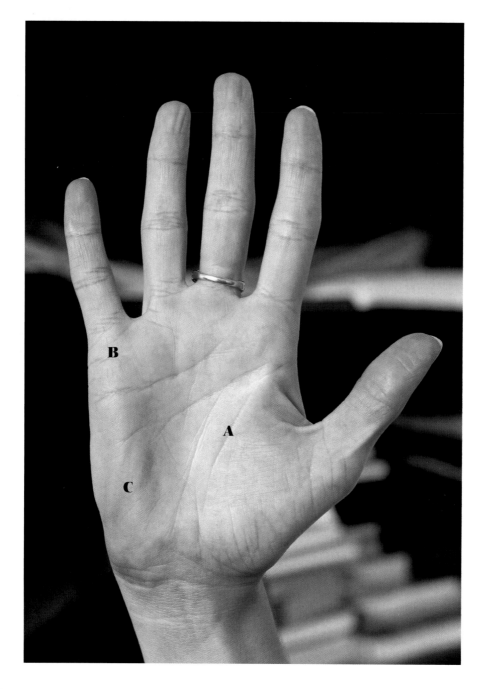

Hand III

There must be one question on this person's mind: "Where?" Their Fire hand indicates a lot of energy and activity, and, as is sometimes the way with this personality type, a certain amount of this energy is often wasted.

Note how this person's Life Line (A) takes a very unusual path, heading more or less straight upward, as opposed to curving signifi-cantly. I suspect that their life has not quite gone according to plan, no matter how much energy they have put into things. This may be the source of some frustration—not least because they probably don't understand why.

The answer may be evident in the distinct "ruffles" between the Mounts of Mercury (B) and The Moon (C): the lines of communication here are rather bumpy. Perhaps this person simply needs to take more time in order to make sure that the message is understood before they rush headlong into the next thing in their life.

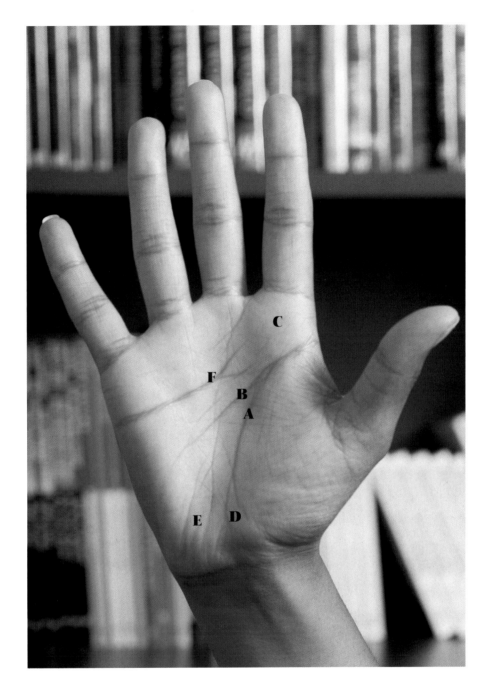

Hand IV

Some survive through hard work, others through determination, and others still through their wit and intellect. The owner of this hand seems to fall into the third category.

The Life (A) and Head Lines (B) intersect, running together for some distance. This shows the progress of life being influenced by their decisions and their actions. The strong Mount of Jupiter (C) implies ambition, which is aided by the slight raising in Neptune (D).

The Mount of The Moon (E) is made up of many ridges, which makes me wonder if this person is the kind that has a million ideas a day. This can be a bad thing, but here perhaps not, as this person seems to have the intellect to sift through and make use of the better ones.

The fork on the Heart Line (F) is an indication that this person might find it a little hard to adjust to partnering with another, unless they apply some more of their natural intelligence to help make it work.

THE ANCIENT RUNES

YOUR LIFE CAST IN STONE?

Go back to your childhood and recall the time spent playing in your garden or perhaps a day at the beach. I am not really a gambling man but I'll bet you used to play with pebbles and stones, perhaps making small piles or laying them out in lines and patterns. You were not the first to be intrigued and mystified by these small pieces of rock, because many ancient cultures found value in them as objects of beauty and currency. Some began to adapt stones in order to be able to discriminate between different values. This, as we have already seen, underlies the development of so many things we take for granted, such as coins, cards, dominoes, and even chess pieces.

I want to introduce you to a particular set of stones, which originate from the ancient Germanic and Nordic cultures. The designs are nowhere as intricate and complex as those on Tarot cards, for example. However, as you look through this next chapter, you will see that rune stones have a real earthy beauty and natural appeal.

THE ORIGINS & HISTORY OF RUNE STONES

Ancient Norse mythology tells us that the whole universe was supported by the World Tree or Yggdrasil (*ig-draz-il*). Its branches supported the world and formed the canopy of the skies whilst the roots extended down into the underworld, the Land Of Giants, and Asgard, the home of the gods.

Odin, the god of wisdom, would be seen riding in the sky astride an eight-legged horse, the light of the sun reflecting in his single blue eye.

It is said that Odin, in order to gain enlightenment, hung for some nine days from the branches of Yggdrasil, impaled by his own sword, gazing upon the runes that lay scattered around him.

From there the legend was born and there have been many variants of the runes through the centuries. The runes we know of today consist of 25 small stones or pieces of wood engraved with the letters of the Germanic alphabet dating from around 200–300AD.

The runes that the ancient Norse used were made by burning the symbols on to small pieces of wood or by marking small pebbles or stones. The ancient Norse would use these runes to determine a diverse range of things: their military strategies, for example, or the best time at which to plant or harvest crops according to what the runes said would happen with the weather.

USING RUNE STONES FOR YOURSELF

Sets of runes can be easily found in New Age stores, and they are usually packaged in a suitable velvet-style purse. They should also have a booklet or guide explaining how they are to be used.

If you wish to, you can make your own set using pebbles (make sure they are flat), tablets of wood, or even heavy card. Mark one side of each with the designs shown in this book.

Over the last 20 years or so I have collected some seven different sets of runes in different materials and different styles. I have grown to favor the set used in the photographs—it is a very modern set but the stones have a real earthy feel about them.

I keep this set in their purse, placed on a shelf just above my eye level, when seated at my writing desk. This serves as a reminder that the runes are there and that it only takes a moment to draw a single stone for a view on the

day ahead. I don't tend to make decisions based upon my rune readings, but I do allow them to set me thinking, to make me pause and reflect.

Thus, in a similar way to Tarot cards, we use them for self-analysis: that is what we ought to guide any querrant or sitter to do with any information we might divine for them.

Runes can be used in two main ways. They can be cast or thrown, and the complex patterns they form analyzed. This is wonderful to do but very time consuming and intricate to learn. It is much simpler and more rewarding simply to draw a small handful of stones for interpretation. Thus I include for your benefit three basic layouts which are my own

variations on some of the classic published systems of reading runes.

In the many books on the subject, one thing that has always confused me is the variation in the names given to each symbol. This has arisen because the alphabet in question has been used for centuries over such a wide area and, of course, time and various dialects have come into play, slowly changing the spellings. I have seen up to eight names for just one symbol.

However, to make it easy for you I have given you 2–4 of the most common names for each, along with a simple meaning. I have also included my own longer interpretation.

Beware that some runes have reversed meanings; others that are symmetrical do not. Typically, a reversed rune indicates a warning that something may not happen or that the element in question need to be sought out or further understood.

Fehu, Feoh, Fe, Fiu: Possessions, cattle, the reward for effort

Have you heard the saying, "The other man's grass is always greener"? Or have you ever heard someone say of another, "She doesn't realize how lucky she is"? These expressions reflect what *Fehu* tells us: to look into ourselves and appreciate what is there, what we have achieved, and most importantly, to preserve and protect our inner wealth.

Uruz, Ur: Strength, courage, individual freedom

"No pain—no gain!" I am sure you know that to get fit you have to work for it. *Ur* reminds us that perhaps we should put more effort into achieving what we desire and that sometimes there is dark before we see the light.

Thurisaz, Thorn, Thi: A gateway, journey or transition

"Look before you leap," my mother always used to warn me and so does *Thi*. Do not rush in and grab every change without taking the time to contemplate the ramifications. If you can be cautious, then you will pass though the transition with more strength and energy.

Ansuz, Ansur, Ansus, Os:
A signal or message

"Many a true word is spoken in jest" and indeed *Ansur* has a strong association with Loki, the mischievous god. So we are warned not to dismiss any message, even if it comes from someone we would not trust, or from an unexpected source.

Kanu, Cen, Kenaz, Kaunaz:
Light and inspiration, leadership

"Hindsight is always 20/20" Given an opportunity to look back and see things more clearly, we can all focus on what matters, on our strength and destiny. We can also push trivial matters into the back-ground and allow ourselves to move forward.

Gebo, Gipt, Giba:
A gift or exchange, partnership

"No man is an island" and we must remember that partnerships build our strength. We must, of course, be careful not to allow our individuality to be suffocated. Mutual gain is achieved through truly balanced relationships.

Raido, Raidho, Rad:
A journey, a coming together

"Seek and ye shall find." However, *Rad* asks us to look beyond ourselves for answers and for direction. We need not be a tower of strength: others may hold something we need. We must be sure to take the right path, not the one we assume is right.

Wyn, Wynn, Wunjo:
Joy and harmony, light and success

Wyn represents a "forbidden fruit." It asks us to be thankful and joyous at seeing the products of our labors but warns us not to consume these benefits in haste. Rather, we should recognize our own ability to nurture and create success and take this forward as we grow further.

Nyd, Nauthiz:
Inner need, pain,
a dangerous path

Are you a "Dr. Jekyll" or a "Mr. Hyde"? The truth is that we are all a mixture of good and bad, strengths and weaknesses, light and shadow. If we fail to recognize this, we will not feed the needs of our whole soul and will not flourish. *Nyd* reminds us to take care of our whole being and that not doing so may hold us back.

Haegl, Hagalaz, Hagl:
Disruption, the unexpected,
the elements at work

"When it rains, it pours." In this case, it hails (for this is how we pronounce the name of this rune). *Haegl* reminds us that sometimes forces beyond our control are at work. The acts of these forces can often be our wake-up call and we must learn from them rather than fight them.

Is, Eis, Isa:
Immobility, ice

Are you "running on ice," not able to make significant progress? This rune symbolizes ice, and you may find yourself on a slippery path, so stop struggling to make progress, for it is futile. Wait for the thaw to come before moving on.

Jera, Jer:
Harvest, a year

"There is a time and a place for everything," and *Jer* reminds of this. If we nurture our crop we may reap when the harvest is due. However, we must not rush things because our yield may not be what we expect.

Eoh, Eihwaz:
Defence, death

"You cannot escape the inevitable," especially if you continue to work hard against it. Some things are immovable, such as our eventual passing over, and yet some of us work so hard against these forces that we cause an early closure. Take a step back, or sidewise, and see if there is another path.

Algiz, Eohl, Eolh:
Protection, a hiding place

"Physician health thyself," for who better than to look after our own well–being than ourselves. Call upon those around you to assist and give you guidance. *Algiz* reminds us that ultimately you are your own responsibility.

Peorth, Perth, Pairthra:
Chance, initiation, a hidden secret

"God moves in mysterious ways" and *Peorth* sits firmly alongside Heaven, indicating other forces at play. They may be hard to see and even more difficult to influence. Expect the unexpected!

Sigel, Sowilo, Sowelu:
Wholeness, victory

"The whole is greater than the sum of its parts," and your journey must end with this completion. Know who and what you are, and share this with everyone around. Express your wholeness and the great prize will be yours.

Teiwaz, Tiwaz, Tyr:
A warrior, justice

"You gotta fight for your rights," but a wise general does not rush into battle. He takes time knowing a good strategy and patience will win in the end. He is also aware that battles are fought by generals and that fate actually controls the outcome.

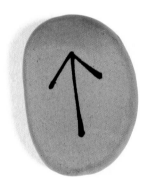

Berkana, Beorc:
Growth, renewal, a tree

"You reap what you sow" reminds us that there is a cycle to life. We know from the concept of Karma that our actions in life, good or bad, will return to us magnified many times. Thus *Beroc* reminds us to undertake our tasks in life with diligence and clarity.

Ehwaz, Eh:
Progress, a journey

"One step at a time." Some people love to drive sports cars really fast, zipping up and down through the gears. They get from A to B quickly, yet frankly nowhere in life. Be more like the long-distance lorry driver, stepping up and down through many gears, adjusting your pace of life to suit the moment.

Lagu, Laguz:
Water, flow

"Go with the flow." Wash away those old thoughts and ways. Leave yourself fresh and ready to take on new challenges. More importantly, look inside yourself and let what lies within flow outward for the benefit of all.

Manna, Mannaz, Man:
Self, friendship, partnership, the intellect

"Modesty is the best policy." Be discreet about your inner self with all but your closest friends. Listen to your mind and your heart in equal balance and make an intelligent judgment against your own impulses.

Ing, Ingwaz, Inguz:
Fertility and birth, family protection

"Keep it in the family," for it is a tight and complete unit that allows for completion and new beginnings. The time is now and, with the protection of this rune, you can achieve what is needed for the good of all.

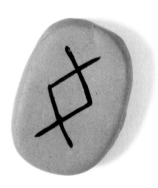

Daeg, Dagaz, Dag:
Day and daylight, breakthrough

"Let the sun shine in" and let it illuminate what is around you. Perhaps you will now see what you must seize and what you have with you. Perhaps this represents a new dawning for you.

Odel, Othala, Ethel:
Inheritance, homeland, separation

"I am my Father's son," but I know I am my own man also. We inherit so much from our families and our ancestors that is of value and importance, but perhaps we tend to cling too tightly for our own good. *Odel* suggests we break free and grow in our own right.

Blank:
Unknown, Odin

This is a most unusual rune, and the meaning is often unclear. This is perhaps because it is a relatively new addition, joining the set perhaps a millennium after they were conceived. I see it is an unknowable question, a sign that we are fallible humans and that there are limits to what we should seek to know.

READINGS FROM THE RUNES

**I find runes a great source of inspiration and so,
in wanting to pass this inspiration to you, I gathered together
a group of people who volunteered to let me carry out
readings for them.**

For our readings I chose to have runes drawn from their purse and laid out in formation. More traditionally, the runes would be thrown or cast and then read; as I mentioned earlier, this is perhaps a little too involved for the beginner.

One of the more fascinating uses of runes that I have read about is a simple game of fate typically played by Norse warriors.

The game, called *Runhalle* (rune-hall-ah), involved repeatedly casting the stones on the floor or table. I suspect the name has evolved over time along with the symbolism associated with the stones. Nonetheless, it seems to have been a very important ritual for them and a vital tool in defining battle strategies and so on.

As the stones were cast, those which fell facing downward were removed and placed back in the purse. The stones would be cast again and

again until only one was left facing upward.

Several people would play it at a time, each taking their turn, and they would each retain their final stone. When everyone present had taken their turn, the stones would be compared and the person with the most senior or appropriate stone would thus be chosen for a particular task. For example he might "win" the honor to lead his compatriots into battle, or he may be given the first choice of any valuables they had won or plundered in battle.

I am sure that you share the wonderful vision of the game being played around the fire at night, and yet we have to remind ourselves that fortune telling is not competitive.

I had the opportunity to meet with an interesting group of volunteers, and offered them a chance to see what the runes had to say!

1. THE SINGLE–RUNE DRAW

This is a quick and simple reading, which can either be used to give a short answer to a question or used as a "thought for the day."

Ask your querrant to shake the purse gently and then hold it open so they may draw a single stone. Have them concentrate on a question to be answered as they do so.

Have them lay the stone on their hand or on a table. Do not make them lay it in any particular direction (other than to lie it symbol–side up of course), as it is important that you allow them subconsciously to lay the stone upright or reversed themselves.

John

John just wanted to know about his situation in life right now. He drew *Mannaz*, and I asked him if there were any decisions that he needed to make at the moment. He indicated that there were and that they were related to a new situation he had found himself in. I suggested that this was a new relationship and he smiled in confirmation.

I suggested that *Mannaz* was advising him to use a policy of slow steps combined with definite communication in order to ensure a positive outcome.

2. THE THREE–RUNE DRAW

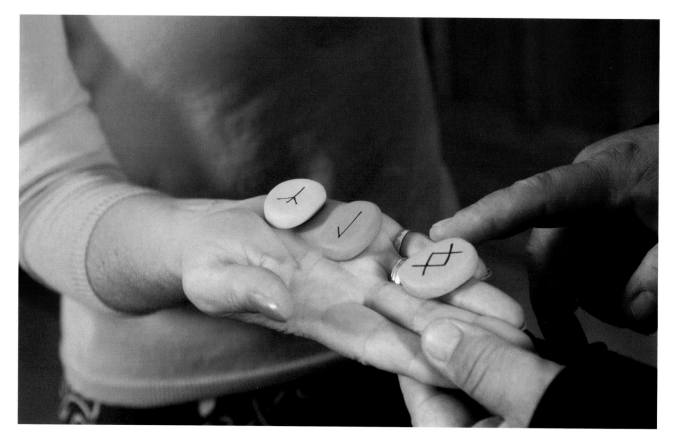

As before, ask your querrant to mix up the runes with a simple light shake of the purse and then draw three stones, one at a time, laying them from right to left on the table in front of them or in their hand.

These three runes will represent past events, forces around you now and opportunities for the future.

Celia

Celia was a most interesting person to read. She had much in her past and present to ponder and many questions about the future for which she wanted answers.

From her right she drew *Algiz*, *Lagu*, and *Ing*. The first two were drawn reversed.

Algiz is the symbol of protection. However, I suspected from the reversed position of the rune that Celia had perhaps allowed herself to be hurt by opening up to other people too readily.

More interesting was *Lagu*, which indicated Celia's current position. This symbol reminds us to go with the flow, but I felt that, in the reversed state, it implied that she was unhappy with changes that might be going on around her. Perhaps these changes seemed out of her control—for example, because they were coming from outside her normal circle of trusted friends.

This seemed to hit home for Celia and she asked what might happen for the future. I was able to give some good indications: *Ing*, the sign of fertility and the family, tells me that she has an opportunity to grow out of these troubled times, provided she realizes that strength lies in herself and in her family, and to make her own judgments.

Celia pondered for a moment and wanted to know some more. I promised her a more detailed reading using cards later in the day. I could tell that she was looking forward to it!

3. THE "WHOLE-WORLD" DRAW

Alex

After my reading for Celia, I met Alex, who was a work colleague of John's. Initially he was a little reticent but, after I had spoken with him for a few minutes, he became more relaxed and I had him draw five stones.

The first rune should be placed in the middle of the table and the remaining four placed around it in a clockwise direction starting from bottom right.

The middle stone represents "You"— in Alex's case, this was *Gebo*. This is a stone of partnership and togetherness. Alex was happy in his current relationship and the stone had confirmed that.

The next stone represents "Home," and here Alex had *Mannaz*, which is a stone of inner reflection and discretion. I suggested to him that perhaps he needs to be more outward looking and not so dependent on home comforts. He seemed unsure but the little shift in his body language gave me the necessary confirmation.

The third stone is about "Work." I wondered if Alex felt he was not making progress at work as he had drawn *Isa*: in fact, he had not been employed there for very long and was keen to make more progress.

The next stone is about "Other Things"— leisure and other activities, for example. Alex chose *Kanu* but reversed. He had done some studying in the past and I felt that *Kanu* was asking him to take up some more educational activities soon to prevent what he had learned already being lost.

Finally, the stone representing "Opportunity" —in this case *Laguz*, which seemed to confirm the other stones in a curious way. Alex was a little reserved and I wondered if overall he was holding himself back in life. Perhaps his opportunity was to jump into the river of life and go with the flow!

CARTOMANCY

THE FUTURE ON THE CARDS?

I have a deck of cards in my hands for at least two hours a day. But then
they are the tools of my trade as a working magician.
Most homes will have at least one deck of cards somewhere. Quite often they will be
found lurking in the back of a drawer somewhere, possibly missing the odd card or
two! Go find yours now. Take a look at the cards one at a time—in particular, look
at the Court cards (the Jacks, Queens, and Kings). I'll bet you have never noticed
all the subtleties in design and the little differences between the suits.
The history of cards is extremely complex and controversial, but the one thing
we can be sure of is that the cards in use today are a reflection of the history and
culture from which they originate. No wonder then that ordinary folk have
seen them as a suitably familiar and useful tool for making predictions.
This chapter introduces us to a little of the history of cards and
their use in fortune telling.

THE ORIGINS & HISTORY OF CARTOMANCY

When Chinese Emperor Mu-Tsung played a game of dominoes using pieces made out of that "newfangled" paper, he probably didn't realise the significance of the moment. However, the event was recorded and we thus have one small clue in an enormous jigsaw puzzle.

Many cultures, but in particular those in the East, developed various "tokens," which they would use to trade, gamble and play games with each other. Often these tokens were made out of small pieces of wood, painted stones, and coins.

Other aspects of the history of playing cards are not so well documented, and the relationship between playing cards, their arrival in Europe, the development of Tarot, and the origins of the suits and Court cards we know today is very confused. There is, however, much research material available and it makes for a fascinating subject.

For the purposes of this book I can offer a short history.

Numerous cultures took to playing games with the stones and coins tokens as far back as several centuries before Christ. Over time, these games became ever more complex, and different values were assigned to different playing pieces in each of these games. Hence, the tokens they were given a number of dots—rather like the dominoes we know today.

In the 10th century, paper became available and the Chinese started making the first types of playing card out of this new material. Typically these "cards" were long thin strips decorated with dots, then later coins, and coins threaded onto a cord.

Around the 13th century, these made their way into Europe, along with another system of cards originating from the Islamic world. These used a

four suit system not unlike the one we use today. Playing cards were introduced to the Americas thanks to explorers such as Columbus and Cortez. The Spanish influence remained strong.

The origin of the Court cards, on the other hand, is less clear. Some say they were first seen in those Islamic cards, others suggest they were an attempt to have permanent Trump or "Triomphe" cards in the deck.

Ultimately, cards reflected the social situation in which they were created and the games people chose to play with them. So it was often the case that Court cards were decorated with caricatures of royalty and politicians, sometimes parodying scandals of the time.

What we are left with today is a plethora of games systems that are derived from those early tokens. So playing cards, dominoes, Mah-Jong, and even Tarot cards have a common root.

In many European decks, the Ace of Spades is particularly ornate. This is a throwback to the days when playing cards were heavily taxed by governments. Each deck had to be stamped to prove the that levy had been paid and, as the Ace of Spades was the highest ranking card (in the game of bridge), it was the natural choice.

In the last two centuries, the 52-card deck we know has become the standard in most parts of the western world, especially for those who play bridge and poker. In some parts of Europe, there are 56-card decks, there being an additional Court card—the Knight—in each suit.

There are various versions of the suits, which all correlate as you can see from this chart.

INTERNATIONAL CARD COMPARISONS

English	Clubs	Hearts	Spades	Diamonds	Jack	Queen	King
German	Acorns/ Crosses	Hearts	Leaves	Bells	Bube	Dame	König
Spanish	Sticks	Cups	Swords	Gold/ Coins	Paje	Reina	Rey
Italian	Rods	Cups	Swords	Money	Fante	Dama/ Regina	Re
French	Trefoils/ Clovers	Hearts	Pikes	Diamonds	Valet	Dame	Roi
Tarot	Wands/ Batons	Cups	Swords	Pentacles/ Coins	Knight	Queen	King

USING CARDS FOR FORTUNE TELLING

Choosing a set of Tarot cards should be a serious business because there is so much diversity and artistry in the many decks available. Playing cards, however, are much more commonplace and essen–tially bland. So it is most definitely acceptable to use any deck that you have at home, or cards that belong to a friend at their home.

There are three simple points I would offer as guidance:
- Make sure that the deck is complete.
- Make sure that it is relatively clean.
- Try to avoid decks that are excessively pictorial—especially those with images carrying any sexual connotations! This is not for prudish reason, but purely because it is important to focus on the cards and their meanings.

There are a wide range of ways to lay out cards for giving readings, and even more, it seems, sets of meanings for each card. These can often be complex and very confusing indeed.

Over the last 25 years or so I have developed my own set of meanings which I am sharing with the rest of the world for the first time in this book. I have tried to make it simple and logical and, in a sense, I have let the cards themselves tell me what they mean.

SUIT MEANINGS

Clubs:
This suit represents the physical aspects of life, such as strength and leadership, dependency, and loyalty.

Hearts:
The more emotional aspects of life are represented by Hearts: for example, home, family, security, and love.

Diamonds:
Diamonds are representative of reward and the pursuit of wealth, along with outside influences, such as work and other associations.

Spades:
Nobody gets something for nothing, and Spades indicate a need for energy, focused effort and work, or potential troubles ahead.

CARD MEANINGS

Ace: The self, your inner thoughts

The Ace asks us to concentrate on who we are and how we feel about our situations, and how we will be affected by what lies ahead or what is already on its way.

Two: A relationship or partnership

We cannot exist alone, and the Two tells us about our relationships—not only with our lovers, but also business and other similar partnerships.

Three: Luck or opportunity

Three is a magic number, for it brings luck and opportunity. Sometimes we need help spotting our chances in life. The Three is there to let us know that opportunity knocks!

Four: Your friends or colleagues

Four represents our "friends" and "colleagues." Although we usually get on well with both groups, we often need to bite our lip for the sake of good order and peace.

Five: A gathering or meeting

Man is a social animal and he is usually to be seen with others. However, Five indicates a gathering that is not simply run of the mill. The question is whether this a cause for celebration or a cause for concern?

Six: Unwelcome influences

At some points in our lives, all of us can be easily led. Some of us, however, are much easier to manipulate than others. Sadly, some of us can even lead ourselves astray. Six serves as a reminder of our own weakness.

Seven: Luck or chance, or perhaps a risky gamble

Sometimes you have to stick your neck out to get what you want in life. At other times you may make a decision without realizing all the implications. Seven is the number of risk and luck—both good and bad!

Eight: Your family

They have seen you grow up and been there for you at those important times. Or perhaps you wish you had been born into a different situation. Eight reminds us that our family play a great part in our lives—like it or not.

Nine: Conflict or dissatisfaction

Why can't people just get along ? Well, because we are all human and so bad at communicating with each other. Nine reminds us that life does not always run smoothly, and that fights or arguments will often occur.

Ten: Plenty or an excess

When is enough really enough? How do we know when we have we had too much? Ten can let us know when we may receive what we need and warn us against taking more than we genuinely require.

Jack: A male influence or father figure

Give some thought to any men who have recently come into your life.

Queen: A female influence or mother figure

Perhaps this is an aunt, a nurse, or simply a caring friend.

King: A leader

Think about who is in charge. Your boss? Your team leader? Or maybe some other figure of authority, such as a priest or doctor?

CARD & SUIT COMBINATIONS

This system is designed to make understanding specific cards very straightforward. It is easy to take the number of the card and put it in context with the meaning of the suit.

Let us look at a few examples—I am sure you will get the idea!

For example, an Ace typically relates to the self. If our Ace is a Club, we might interpret this as indicating that we are, or that we need to be, strong for someone else around us. If the Ace is a Heart, however, it indicates a love of our own self. More often, it implies a need to love ourselves more fully.

Sixes indicate unwelcome influences. If it is a Six of Spades, this might indicate problems at work, whereas a Six of Diamonds might warn of unexpected financial demands.

Kings imply a leader or a guiding influence. Thus a King of Spades indicates a presence of a manager or perhaps a sporting coach. Conversely, a King of Diamonds implies a financial expert or adviser of some sort.

The real secret is seeing and interpreting sequences of cards. Only then does the whole picture start to become visible.

The Joker?

I prefer not to use the Joker in my readings. I find him a distraction and he is often not even present in some older decks of cards. It is possible, if you so wish, to use him as a "wild" card that represents something unknown or something your querrant has to decide for themselves—it's up to you!

CARTOMANCY READINGS

When I did a reading for her using runes, I was intrigued by the response I received from Celia. I wanted to know more and offered her a reading with my cards. I was also fortunate enough to meet with some of her friends who also agreed to let me read their cards.

For all card readings it is, rather obviously, much better for both you and your querrant to be sitting at a table or, alternatively, making use of another suitable clean surface on which to lay the cards. Try and sit opposite your querrant as this will enable you to orient your–self easily, because the position of the cards is most important.

Begin by having your querrant mix the cards. Try to keep this to an overhand shuffle, rather than riffling the cards together—most people do that badly and, quite frankly, it ruins the cards over time! Have them think about themselves, their lives, and any pertinent questions as they shuffle.

Then direct them to lay the cards in order for the particular spread that you intend to use.

1. THE THREE-CARD SPREAD

Other than choosing a single card, this is perhaps the most simple of the "meaningful" card readings one can give.

Celia, for whom I had done a rune reading, introduced me to Peter and offered him the chance of a reading with me. He was happy to agree.

For this reading, you should have your querrant shuffle the cards and ask them to think about themselves and what is going on in their life. Ask them to stop when they wish and lay out three cards facing down from their right to their left.

As with the runes, these cards represent the past, present, and future. You can now turn the cards over one at a time explaining each as you go.

Peter's "Past" card was the Nine of Spades. A simple interpretation might be unhappiness in the work environment. However, I felt that this was not really the case. In fact, I felt that it was a sign of past frustrations that perhaps were a result of Peter being over-eager to make progress.

This led on to the Ace of Clubs as the "Present," which implied that Peter is now in a position to begin understanding his strengths, allowing him to start using them to his advantage.

Finally for the "Future," we had the Six of Hearts. I wondered if Peter was sometimes torn between leading his own life and his responsibilities to others. He nodded. I felt that as he progressed, those close to him may put pressures on him to make decisions. I suggested that he focus on the Ace of Clubs and realize his own duties to himself, trying to ensure that he keeps his other commitments in balance.

Peter left the reading looking quite intense, and it was apparent that what the cards had suggested rang true for him.

2. THE "WHOLE-WORLD" SPREAD

This is a spread that I have used for a number of years and one I enjoy using the most. As you may have noticed, I have even adapted it for rune readings. I felt that it would be a suitable spread to find out a little bit more about Celia, for whom I had done a rune reading earlier on.

After your querrant has mixed the cards, have them lay one face down in the center of the table and then lay four cards in a clockwise direction around it.

Each of these five cards represents a sphere of activity, influence, or feeling and emotion.

I asked Celia to turn the cards one at a time starting with the center card, which represents the "Sphere of You."

The King of Clubs indicates an important person around Celia, and I was not certain who this was. I was troubled by the Club and asked Celia if she had felt unsettled and perhaps a little battle-weary from those immediately around her.

Then I realized the meaning of the card in this context. It was Celia who had been quite hard on herself lately. I suggested that she could be being too harsh and that I imagined she wasn't really to blame for what happened. She sighed in agreement.

The next card represents the "Sphere of Home"—this relates to family—and it was the Ten of Spades. Thinking back to the previous card, I suggested that although Celia may be wary of some people in her life and what they have done, there was a strong family connection and many people close to her who were supporting her and who wanted to help. Her situation may not be easy, but there was no shortage of energy at hand.

Rather interestingly, the next card was also a Ten—this time a Diamond. This position represents the "Sphere of Work" and it was interesting that it should reveal a diamond, which has work connections. If this had been a black-suited Ten, I might have suggested that it meant there was a

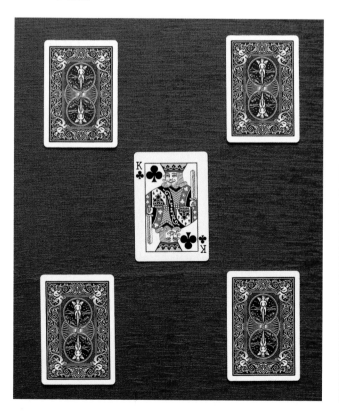

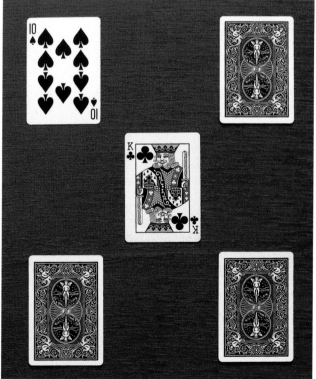

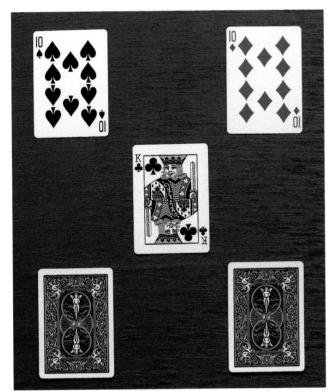

lot of hard work. However, the red suit implied to me a lot of other forces at play. I wondered if there were perhaps changes and moves occurring in the work place.

I could see from Celia's reaction that this was the case, and that this atmosphere was, in fact, causing her to be unsettled.

The third card represents "The Other Sphere," which relates to social activities, pastimes, or perhaps studies. Another Ten—the Ten of Clubs! I was unsure what this truly meant. On the one hand, I felt that Celia was not enjoying life outside work, which she confirmed. On the other, it confirmed the meaning of the Ten of Spades, indicating there was plenty of support for her in her social circles.

Finally, the fourth card, which represents the "Sphere of Opportunity." This yielded the Five of Diamonds, which made me smile a little. For this card, along with the others, seemed to confirm the potential outcome that was indicated by *Ing* in her rune reading.

A Five represents a gathering or coming together. Celia has a family network that is strong, although these have been trying times.

If Celia can find a way to clear away these feelings of self-doubt along with any erroneous influences, and bring the family and friends around her, there is great opportunity for reward.

3. THE "REFLECTING EYE" SPREAD

As you will learn later on, I value enormously the ability of people to sit, ponder, and reflect on life. After dabbling with many card spreads over the years, I came up with this unique spread that has reflection as its inspiration.

Sue asked me to do a reading for her, to help resolve some issues that were on her mind at the time.

For this reading you should ask your querrant to shuffle the cards and hand them to you. Lay out seven cards roughly in the shape of an eye, face downward. The order or starting point is not important in this spread because the positions are not significant.

Next, lay out another seven cards, each one placed face up beneath one of the cards already on the table. These are the reflection cards, and we are predominantly interested in the suits.

Now turn the other cards over one at a time. These give us situations, problems, or concepts to consider, but we must use these in light of the reflection cards. This is best illustrated by looking at the cards that Sue drew.

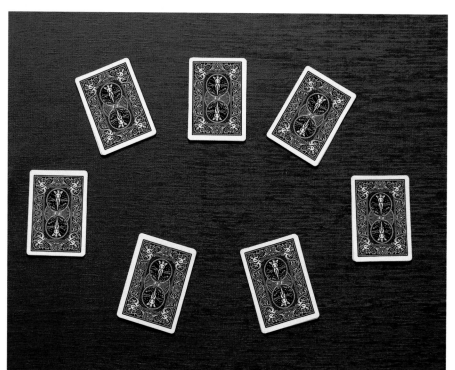

Seven of Diamonds reflected by a Club

Certainly one has to speculate to accumulate. The Seven indicates a gamble or risk of some sort that Sue is about to take. The reflecting Club warns her to be strong and see it through in order to make sure it pays off.

Six of Spades reflected by a Club

There are those around trying to disrupt Sue's working environment—again, the reflecting Club reminds her to "stick to her guns!"

Ace of Hearts reflected by a Diamond

This combination is telling Sue to look after herself and care for her needs—all of her needs. The reflecting Diamond indicates some other dimension of life, perhaps one that she enjoys but has been ignoring.

Four of Spades reflected by a Spade

When both cards are of the same suit it is an indication to take the meaning of the top card very seriously—the matching reflective card reinforces the meaning. The Four in this situation suggests to me that Sue needs to be sure she knows who all her friends are.

Five of Hearts reflected by a Heart

Interestingly, this pair supports the previous cards. Five indicates a gathering and Hearts, of course, are signs of love, family, and security. Perhaps Sue should make sure she doesn't lose sight of the strength of her family.

Seven of Spades reflected by a Club

Again, some reinforcement for Sue. There are decisions and opportunities ahead in the sphere of work and yet the Club is a constant reminder to Sue of the need to be both firm and consistent.

Ten of Diamonds reflected by a Spade

Not too difficult to interpret for Sue. Success at work is the message here, which leads me to the final part of this reading…

The Overall Picture

I see that there are challenges ahead, but I think that Sue is aware of them. When taking risks it is important to know who you can place your trust in; that is not clear to Sue at the moment. And so she must get all her facts straight, look to her own intuition, and allow her friends and family to be there to support and guide her.

THE ANCIENT TAROT

YOUR LIFE SPREAD OUT BEFORE YOU?

Have you ever seen a deck of Tarot cards? If you haven't, have a quick skip through the coming chapter. Don't read the words just yet—just look at the pictures. You have to agree that they are things of true beauty, with so much color and intricate and vibrant designs on every card. Yet this is just one example of one particular card design. If you search the Internet or even go to a store you can find many dozens of different designs, some very old, some more contemporary. Tarot cards share a common history with playing cards, and the designs are ultimately a reflection of the culture they stem from. Tarot cards have always had a more spiritual context and it is perhaps this which has caused them to retain their more complex designs while playing cards have become a little more ordinary.
In this chapter, we learn more about these most beautiful objects and how we can use them for our readings.

THE ORIGINS & HISTORY OF TAROT CARDS

Which came first: the chicken or the egg? Which came first: playing cards or Tarot cards? Both questions seem to provoke debate.

The reality, however, is a little easier to decipher as far as cards are concerned. In fact, it is largely an Anglo–American perspective that has caused the debate, because we have tended to be aware only of our own 52–card deck.

Other cultures, particularly in Europe, have varying quantities of cards in their decks. By tracing their history, it becomes easier to see how the modern Tarot deck derived from the early Italian and Swiss decks of the 13th and 14th centuries. In fact, a modern deck from Italy comprises 56 cards, just like the Minor Arcana from the Tarot.

Perhaps one reason for the belief that the Tarot deck has a longer history is that it contains many ancient references in its design. Aspects of the Qabbalah and "Ancient Mysteries" can be found hidden in the artwork of many Tarot sets. However, these are usually more the result of the artists' interpretation than of any specific historical reference.

It is around the 15th century that we see the first examples of what we would recognize today as a Tarot deck—78 cards divided into two sections:

The Minor Arcana, which consists of 56 Cards in four suits: these are directly comparable to regular playing cards.

The Major Arcana, which consists of 22 cards, each depicting unique image or character, separate from the others. It is believed that these were originally additional Trump or "Triomphe" cards created for card games.

CHOOSING & USING TAROT CARDS

This is a little more involved than choosing a deck of regular cards for fortune telling—it is the artistry and imagery that Tarot readers use to inspire their thoughts and to light that inner spark of enlightenment.

You can see many decks for sale on the Internet, but I recommend going to a store to choose your own. The feel of the deck is just as important as the look and you simply cannot get that sense from an image alone.

Decks are widely available from toy- and bookstores but, if you have one nearby, I would recommend that you visit a New Age store. They will usually have a far greater range and thus you can make a really informed choice about your purchase.

Caring for your cards is important and many Tarot readers recommend wrapping the cards in silk or velvet and storing them carefully in your jewelry box or even your underwear

drawer. The idea is that by being close to your personal things when not in use, they will be recharged with your energies.

There are a few differences between giving readings using Tarot cards and those that employ a "standard" deck.

Firstly, it is recommended that only you handle the Tarot deck. You should gently shuffle the cards and ask your querrant to call, "Stop." You should then lay out the cards in from of you, starting with the top card of the deck.

Also, after the reading, you should gather up the cards and leave them in whatever order they ended up in. The position in which you finish one reading is the starting point for the next. Never sit down after a few readings and put your deck back in order!

Tarot cards are directional, unlike regular cards, and so their orientation is important. Cards that are upside down—"reversed"—tend to have a different interpretation—typically (although not always) the opposite of the "normal" meaning.

Tarot cards take longer to learn to use than playing cards: this is mainly because there are many more definitions and interpretations to understand. Also, as a beginner, you are at a distinct disadvantage, because the cards and suits of a regular deck will be familiar to you. Tarot cards have a whole new world of imagery and meanings to learn and understand. My recommendation is that you start with just the 22 cards of the Major Arcana.

In fact, I know of many Tarot readers who never use the Minor Arcana, as they seem to gain sufficient inspiration from the Major Arcana alone. Ultimately, the key issue with Tarot cards, and indeed any fortune-telling tool, is that you are comfortable with what you use. Thus, I will leave you to decide for yourself as your skills and knowledge develop.

THE MAJOR ARCANA

The Major Arcana consists of 22 cards, each separate with a unique image or character. It is believed that these were originally additional Trump or "Triomphe" cards created for card games.

0: The Fool

Rather like the Joker in a standard deck of cards, the Fool is somewhat of an open traveler who can "fit in anywhere." This adaptability is tied in with his meaning—he encourages us to take on life and go for new challenges as they arise.

But beware! If the Fool comes reversed, we should exercise caution and listen to those around us.

I: The Magician/ The Sorcerer

This brash entertainer is a sign of confidence and success. He performs miracles wherever he goes! His presence is positive and augurs well for the task in hand.

If he is reversed, we are reminded that all is not as it may seem and that we should be cautious of where or in whom we place our trust.

II: The High Priestess

This lady is both beautiful and powerful. Showing great intuition, she is a source of inspiration. Her presence implies some hidden spiritual motivation rather than external materialism. She speaks "from the heart."

When reversed, she warns us not to let our heart rule our head or, worse, be swayed by material thoughts.

III: The Empress

An "Earth Mother," who has a deep, caring soul and seeks to nurture all of those around her. Sometimes she can be a little too overprotective and overpowering. She is often a sign of a solid home life.

If she arrives reversed, we should beware of insecurities and not allow ourselves to lose direction and focus.

IV: The Emperor

The perfect partner to the Empress, this man is a strong and wise father figure. If he turns up for you, the implication is that you have his strength, and that you can fight your corner and are willing to stand your ground.

In a reversed position, he indicates a need of help or guidance from a parent or person of authority.

V: The High Priest or Hierophant

The Priest is a channel for great wisdom and spiritual intuition. He presents us with a gift of inspiration and asks for nothing in return—a great teacher to a willing student.

His reversed side, however, is rather sinister, as he has a rebellious streak and may be deliberately offering misleading advice.

VI: The Lovers

This card is not just about our relationships, but also shows our love of beauty and nature. It reminds us of the care we need to take in our partnerships and the difficult choices we sometimes need to make. Crucially, we should not forget the times our heart has ruled our head.

Conflict is likely if the card is reversed. We may see the end of a long-term commitment.

VII: The Chariot

This card indicates a rushed life, with many aspects all competing for our attention. It tells us to keep our heads and we can succeed in that journey.

Of course, things will come tumbling down around us if we do not keep our cool: when this card is reversed, it is a warning that this may occur.

VIII: Justice

This card reminds us of a need for balance—not just in our judgment of others but in our lifestyle too—and can show a desire to "right wrongs" and help others fight for their rights.

Reversed, the card warns us that we may be judged unfairly by others or that we may find it hard to accept the rule of law. (NB in some decks this is card XI.)

IX: The Hermit

A stubborn old man, the Hermit lives on his own, convinced he is right about everything. Whilst undoubtedly wise, he can be behind the times and not willing to listen to others and their ideas. This card is a warning to us to be aware of what is going on.

Reversed, he warns of the negative aspects of isolation, such as loneliness and paranoia.

X: The Wheel of Fortune

A symbol of the great circle of life and a clear sign of positive change in the here and now. We should not question destiny, but accept the goodness that nature brings forward.

If the Wheel is reversed, then the changes may be for the worst or come at a cost.

XI: Strength

Perhaps not surprisingly, this card is a symbol of strength, courage, and, above all, stamina and determination. The Strength card can also imply a good recovery from ill-health or other disasters.

In a reversed position, it carries implications of weakness and a lack of determination and willpower.

(NB in some decks this is card VIII.)

XII: The Hanged Man

A gruesome sight? Look closer. The man is not hanging dead from his neck, but simply cannot move—suspended by the feet. This might indicate a time when you are unable to make progress because events beyond your control are having a negative influence.

If it is reversed, you should ask yourself if you place too much emphasis on frivolous matters.

XIII: Death

Perhaps the most feared and misunderstood card in the Tarot, it usually signifies something positive! It reminds us that after death there is rebirth and thus signifies change—the end of one phase and the beginning of a new one.

If reversed, it suggests that despite the closing of one door the next may not open readily.

XIV: Temperance

A card of harmony and accord that reminds us to respect others around us, to share what we have and to avoid overindulgence. It is a good sign that our current affairs and concerns will have positive outcomes.

Reversed, it signifies that there may be unrest or quarrels ahead: perhaps others are unhappy about your overindulgences.

XV: The Devil

Why have so many sold their soul to the Devil? Because he has an overwhelming and unyielding power that is incredibly alluring. This card can signify a person with compelling energies or an opportunity that causes you to question your own good morals.

Reversed, this card offers a chance to give up old habits and control your animal urges.

XVI: The Tower

Some say that this is the most negative card in the deck. It depicts a scene of devastation and death brought about by natural forces. That said, there is a positive aspect of opportunity and a chance to rebuild.

If reversed, the calamity may not fall open you, but upon someone else around you.

XVII: The Star

Full of energy, light, and enthusiasm, this card signifies good things coming from any changes that are taking place. It also reminds us that we have untapped skills and energies within ourselves, which we would do well not to overlook.

Are you a little arrogant or overenthusiastic? A reversed Star indicates that others are wary of this side of you.

XVIII: The Moon

The Moon is a symbol of the fanciful and irrational aspects of life. This card can show up when you are feeling confused or uncertain of your abilities. Use it to remind yourself that self-doubt is just a foolish thought and that you can make progress even if you're not sure how.

Reversed, it warns you that you do not always know best!

XIX: The Sun

During the long winter months we all dream of feeling the Sun's warmth again. This is our reward for seeing it through and doing our duty: when this card shines on us, our efforts will bear fruit as long as we are patient.

Reversed, it simply means that we may have to work a little harder and a little longer before we see results.

XX: Judgment

A decision has to be made. Perhaps it is you who has to sit back and analyze the evidence, before you (or maybe someone else) can judge you. No matter, this is a notice to you that the time has come and positive action is required.

If reversed, this card tells of potential dismay about missing out on "what could have been."

XXI: The World

The final fulfillment and completion of what had to be done. The world is now yours and you can rest for a while and move on in due course. It can also portend promotion or travel. In any case, this card is a sure sign of success.

Reversed, this card shows that your success is yet to be realized by others, even though you feel it yourself.

THE MINOR ARCANA

These 56 cards have a direct connection with standard playing cards. The suits are essentially the same, although they have different names and significances. The table on page 60 compares the suits and cards in various types of deck.

Here is a very brief one- or two-word definition for each of these cards. Reversed meanings can be generally seen as just that, the opposite of the definition given.

The Suit of Chalices

Associated with the Suit of Hearts, Chalices are connected to emotional affairs.

One: Love and fertility
Two: Partnership and commitment
Three: Joy and happiness
Four: Emotional excess
Five: Love lost
Six: Memories
Seven: Hope and opportunity
Eight: A search
Nine: Contentment
Ten: Joint achievement
Page: Youthful energy
Knight: A young lover
Queen: Loyalty and faithfulness
King: Caring and sensuality

The Suit of Swords

This suit is comparable to the Suit of Spades and indicates intellectual and physical effort and conflict.

Ace: Success and power
Two: Equality and balance
Three: Despair and heartache
Four: Rest and revitalization
Five: Impending defeat
Six: A journey ahead
Seven: Distrust
Eight: Difficulty and constraint
Nine: Cruelty and pain

Ten: Disaster and destruction
Page: A youthful ally
Knight: A fair-weather friend
Queen: A graceful lady
King: A wise leader

The Suit of Wands

Sometimes known as the Suit of Batons or Rods, this is associated with the Suit of Clubs. This is the suit of endeavor and enterprise.

Ace: Inspiration and enterprise
Two: Joint success
Three: Boldness rewarded
Four: Popularity and success
Five: Challenges and setbacks
Six: Victory and reward
Seven: Continued defiance

Eight: Rapid progress
Nine: Resilient opposition
Ten: A heavy load
Page: A helpful apprentice
Knight: A traveling companion
Queen: A dominant female
King: A determined leader

The Suit of Pentacles or Coins

The suit of Pentacles or Coins is linked with the Suit of Diamonds and is associated with wealth and prosperity.

Ace: Long term prosperity
Two: Financial difficulties
Three: Success and entrepreneurialism
Four: Your possessions
Five: Ruin and poverty
Six: Charity and giving
Seven: The review of plans

Eight: Patience rewarded
Nine: Stability and comfort
Ten: An inheritance
Page: A sensible friend
Knight: An honorable man
Queen: A generous woman
King: A good advisor

TAROT READINGS

**Tarot cards abound in historical richness and cultural diversity.
Their iconography is both beautiful and intriguing.
They can be set out in different spreads—choose the one
that seems most appropriate to your
querrant's situation.**

1. THE "TRISKELE" SPREAD

I met up with Lisa. She had quite a lot going on in her life at the time and was looking for some inspiration as to what course of action she should take in a number of ways. With so much happening, I felt a "Triskele" spread was the ideal choice. It is fairly neat and relatively quick, yet it has a framework that invites the querrant to think intensely about their situation.

The first card in this spread is laid in the middle and is known as "The Covering." It represents the important issues of the moment—in this

case it was Strength, which represents determination and willpower, which I felt indicated Lisa's need to "stay in here" for the time being.

Laid across this is a card know as "The Crossing," which highlights issues and obstacles: in this case it was the Six of Coins. This card indicates giving, and I asked Lisa to consider whether she might be working too hard, with little regard for her own needs.

This seemed to touch a nerve, and so we moved on to the next card, known as "The Root" and placed on the lower left—this card is about the past, and Lisa drew the Four Of Chalices. Perhaps Lisa had exhausted herself in a previous relationship?

Next we have "The Future" card which sits at bottom right—here we have the Tower. This is often a card showing destruction, but I suggested that this might mean the need to clear away what has gone on previously, and allow herself to take back some of the

energy and emotion she has recently allowed to drain away.

The final card represents "The Outcome" and here we have a very positive card—the King of Chalices, which represents care and sensuality. This all seemed to make sense to me and, more importantly, to Lisa, as it seemed she had so much to resolve that it could actually be just a matter of taking more care of herself.

2. THE "CALENDAR" SPREAD

As you begin to give readings to your friends, family, and others, you will find that many of them are unable to find specific questions for the Tarot to answer. Instead, they might simply want to try out a Tarot reading to see what it has to offer them. Most of the time they end up being quite surprised how accurate the reading can be—one such person was my old friend Andrew.

I suggested a Calendar spread for him. It is simple and easy to understand for a first timer, yet pretty comprehensive.

Twelve cards are laid out in a clock-face formation and a thirteenth is laid in the middle.

Each of the cards represent one month in the coming year, beginning from the 1 o'clock position (the first card you laid down). I tend to read three cards at a time, effectively looking at the year by quarters. As with all Tarot readings, it is a good idea not to be too prescriptive in interpreting the meanings, it being better to see how the whole picture builds.

The first quarter for Andrew was very interesting. It began with the Chariot and the Queen of Wands reversed and ended with the Queen of Chalices.

The reversed chariot implies that Andrew needs to keep going ahead with what he is doing or things could break down for the worse. The Queen of Wands shows that there is a strong female influencing Andrew at this time and, because she is reversed, this influence is probably not for the better. However, the Queen of Chalices indicates that, if

he keeps at things, this influence will ultimately prove to be worthwhile and beneficial to him over a longer period of time.

The next quarter gave us the Six of Swords, the Knight of Coins, and the Knave or Page of Coins reversed.

Here we have a journey—perhaps the need to work on finances, as indicated by the coins. I suggested to Andrew that he should seek good financial advice from a professional, as indicated by the Knight, and not a well-meaning but perhaps unqualified friend, as shown by the Knave.

Months seven to nine in the spread gave us nothing but Wands—that is the Eight, Seven, and Nine.

This gave a very strong message to me—namely, if he remains defiant and resilient to the challenges that arise at this time, he will progress through it all the stronger.

Our last quarter gave us the King of Swords reversed, followed by the Queen of Swords and, lastly, the Queen of Coins.

This series of cards indicated some potential conflict that is related to finance around this time, and warned again that he should listen to those in positions of knowledge rather than those to whom he has some sort of emotional attachment.

Having said all that the overall outlook was positive, as indicated by our final card—the King of Chalices—which represents our querrant: a caring man, who has plenty to give, just so long as he watches the influences around him with a careful eye!

3. THE "CELTIC CROSS" SPREAD

I had a long chat with a friend of Lisa's, Graeme, and offered to give him a reading. I suggested that we do the "Celtic Cross"—this is one of the most popular and universally used Tarot spreads and seemed ideal for Graeme, because I found out through talking with him that he has a strong interest in Celtic history and mythology.

In this spread, ten cards are laid out beginning with one in the center. This center card represents the reading itself—setting the tone of the reading and indicating the problems or issues that are relevant to the querrant. The second card is laid across this center card. It represents obstacles or challenges that the querrant is facing, in a similar way to the "Triskele" spread.

For Graeme's reading we had a pair of Wands, namely the Seven first and the Eight second. The Seven told me that this reading was going to be about Graeme sticking to his guns and pursuing his goals no matter what was being thrown at him. He told me that he had recently made a tricky career move and was working hard. This was borne out by the Eight, which represents fast progress and lots of things going on. I wondered whether all this activity was a risk and if he needed to take more care.

The third card in the sequence—the Nine of Chalices—at the bottom, shows the querrant's true and perhaps hidden feelings about the situation. This is balanced by card five—here the Ten of Swords—at the top, which concerns the querrant's known thoughts and feelings. These two cards need to be considered together.

The latter represents failure or disaster, and I wondered if Graeme sometimes failed to shout out to the world about his success, for the Nine of Chalices indicated that he was happy—he had moved into a world where he was naturally at peace.

Now to card four on the left, which was the Nine of Wands. This tells us of some of the past

issues related to our querrant. I asked Graeme if he had been in a situation in the past where he had been unhappy at work and had to battle with unhelpful colleagues and difficult bosses. His response was "All the time!"

But what could be said of the future? This is given by the card to the right at position six—the Queen of Chalices. Chalices always imply love and fulfillment, and the Queen shows us a chance for long term success and benefits: a good sign indeed.

Graeme drew the Death card in position seven at the bottom of the line. This always scares people when it turns up, but usually unnecessarily. This position represents the querrant himself and the card was, in fact, reversed. I felt compelled to take Graeme back to cards representing his internal and external feelings, because Death reversed means that although good changes are coming, the querrant may not be ready. Perhaps more acknowledgment of his success would open the door to even more opportunities.

The next card up represents the querrant's environment, either physical or emotional. The card drawn here was the Empress reversed. The signals were coming ever more loud and clear to me, because this provides a warning to the querrant not to let his insecurities hinder his progress.

The penultimate card deals with the querrant's hopes and fears. Here we have the High Priestess reversed. This lady always tells us to be true to our hearts and again warns us to be clear of mind. Graeme nodded and told me he was "getting the message."

Our last card shows what our final outcome may be and here Graeme drew the Seven of Chalices. If you look back at the definition I gave for this card you will see two words which truly sum up everything the rest of this reading gave Graeme—hope and opportunity.

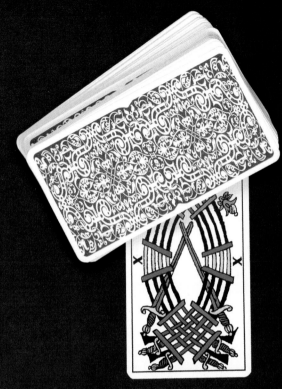

SCRYING & CLAIRVOYANCE

THE FUTURE IN PERSPECTIVE?

Where do you go to think? When life is getting on top of you and you can't clear
your head, what do you do to step outside the hustle and bustle of life?
We have found many methods of chilling out over the millennia—some effective, some
not so, and some just plain dangerous! Some of us pollute our bodies in order to relax
by using alcohol, cigarettes, and other drugs. One of the most famous "seers" in history,
Michel de Nostredame (aka Nostradamus) is reputed to have had his visions whilst
under the influence of mind-altering drugs.
So was all this really necessary? They may have found a means of exploring their
inner psyche and perhaps solved some personal issues and even "seen the future,"
but at what cost to their health?
The answers to most of our problems are there for us to see—we just need to
find a way to get them out. In this chapter we look at how scrying and
contemplation may show us the way to see clearly what lies ahead.

TRULY SEEING BEYOND

Scrying, the art of divination by gazing upon reflective surfaces, is known to have been practiced for at least 7,000 years.

During that time mankind has found many different things to focus upon while scrying. The ancient Babylonians, for example, would massage oil into their fingernails and gaze for hours, letting their mind wander and seek out answers.

In other times, the priest or seer would fill cups or bowls with a solution of oil and soot. This would create a deep reflective black surface with no apparent end, which was ideal for scrying.

In fact, it appears that most civilizations have scried in one form or another, be it with crystal balls (crystallomancy), water (hydromancy), fire (pyromancy), or from within their own minds.

So what was it that the practitioners of scrying could actually do with this marvelous skill? Some would claim to see the future, some the past; others would claim to see what was happening at that very moment in far away places. Whatever they claimed to be able to see, most scriers had one common belief: they knew that what they could see reflected back to them was reality.

I recall reading somewhere recently that, at the peak of the Cold War, the KGB employed more psychics than it did active spies. This may be just the stuff of urban legend. However, it is known that various covert organizations have frequently turned to those with more mystical powers to try to give them an edge in the counterintelligence battle.

Thus, with "Government Approval" there must be something of the truth in what can be "seen"—it all seems to make sense, doesn't it?

Once again, my personal view is potentially controversial but does at least give credibility to the subject.

For me, scrying and clairvoyance (the ability to "see" remotely) are closely linked with the art of meditation. If employed correctly, we have a wonderful skill at our disposal that can enable us to sort through, clarify, and order our thoughts and allow us the opportunity to see life from an alternative perspective.

So by relaxing and focusing we can indeed "see" remotely, albeit not a remote reality. Our mind is more than capable of working out problems, predicting outcomes, and even accurately imagining what is happening elsewhere—we just need to find a way to unlock that potential.

And so, in this chapter, we will explore how to combine scrying and some contemplative skills that will enable you to find solutions to problems and gain insight into the outcomes that may await you.

SCRYING FOR YOURSELF

I first tried to "see" beyond my immediate physical domain when I was 11 or 12 years old. I would lie in bed, breathe deeply, and let myself wander through my mind. I do not know for certain why I did this. Of course I was almost a teenager with all the pain and angst that the hormonal changes in your body bring. There had been trials and recent traumas in my life at that time, and perhaps I was simply seeking to

put those issues to rest. Whether or not I actually saw anything that was in another place is, I firmly believe, irrelevant. What I began to discover was that I could see answers to problems and solutions to difficult situations if I took the time to contemplate and focus.

A few years later, I found an old book on how to teach yourself to be clairvoyant. In fact, what it taught was how to scry and relax, in order to let answers come forward by themselves. What I began to realize was that this skill is neither fanciful nor magical. It is, in fact, pure common sense. More specifically, it seemed to be a way of clearing the mind of irrelevance and letting clarity and reality prevail.

In those days, I would scry into my bedroom mirror—not an ideal surface, but at least it was one with which I was familiar. Later in life, I dabbled further with scrying, having been given a crystal ball as a gift by a good friend. This helped me focus far more easily, especially when I began to use the exercises I will share with you later in this chapter. Nowadays, I see my crystal ball as a wonderful ornament, which I use for scrying occasionally. There are, however, two places in which I tend to scry: one in my home and the other outside, although not far away.

At home, I gaze upon a glass-paneled door that leads to another glass-paneled door that leads to the light of day and the shadows of the night. The combination of the two patterns forms a myriad of shapes and images in my mind. I can see that door as I sit at my desk writing. I use these doors to give me inspiration when I suffer with that cursed writer's block!

Not far from my home is a river, a stretch of water with a long history and a wide variety of scenery from the dirty and industrial to the serene and tranquil. I sometimes sit on the wall or just pause on the footbridge and gaze into the ripples. There I can sometimes find solutions to problems and answers to questions.

You may be wondering why I am telling you so much about how I scry. This is because it is such a personal thing and I want you to find the right place and a good surface to gaze upon for inspiration. I hope that by showing you some of what has inspired me you will be equally awoken to what suits you. There is, frankly, a lot of confusing and unnecessary information given about the choice of objects or surfaces with which to scry. The key, however, is that it feels right and works for you.

By all means, purchase a crystal ball if you wish. They are readily available in New Age stores, but they do not come cheap. That said, they are quite beautiful to behold, whether you use them for scrying or just as an ornament.

It is often said that you must choose one that is free from imperfections. I am not convinced that this is overly important; it certainly is less significant than your own awareness of the impurities that are there. If you know they are present they can become important friends as you scry: indeed, they will help remind you of one most important facet of your own character—your own imperfections and shortcomings!

But there are other objects you can use which may be at your home. Mirrors, windows, vases, or even a garden pond can be used. The most important thing you can do is be comfortable with what you are using, especially as you are learning how to scry.

THE SCRYING PROCESS

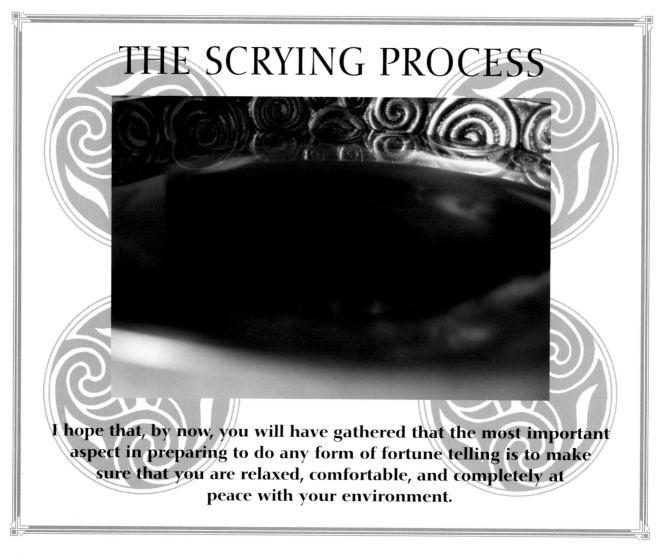

I hope that, by now, you will have gathered that the most important aspect in preparing to do any form of fortune telling is to make sure that you are relaxed, comfortable, and completely at peace with your environment.

This is even more important when scrying and it is very helpful if you can avoid other distractions. Turn off the television and your phone, perhaps draw your curtains and think about your timing—are you likely to be inter-rupted by visitors? Position yourself so that you can see your crystal ball, water, or other scrying surface easily and that it is central to your field of vision.

Close your eyes—not tightly—and take a deep breath in through your nose, slowly releasing the air through your mouth. Repeat this twice—three breaths in all. As you breathe, try to let your mind clear. It may help to envis-age a cloudy sky and feel the clouds blow away through your mouth as your breathe out. Now open your eyes slowly and gaze onto your

scrying surface (do not stare intensely as this will tire your eyes). Let yourself find a point in the center to concentrate on. Keep your focus fixed on the surface, letting your peripheral vision become aware of the outer edge. Continue to breathe deeply and let the outer edge grow around you, until it envelops you completely.

This may take some practice to get right but, with a little effort, you will begin to feel your-self almost totally immersed in your surface. Let yourself remain in that state of immersion for a few minutes. Let your thoughts wander, flitting to and from wherever they choose. Most importantly, enjoy the moment, because you should be feeling warm, relaxed, and at ease. Now close your eyes one more time and take

three deep gentle breaths as before. On the last one, breathe out very slowly, letting your eyes open. Now be aware of the room around you. Sit and relax for a few more moments before rising from your seat or moving onto something else.

What we have just learned is, of course, just practice to prepare yourself to scry for real. That said, there is not a great deal more to say on the subject in itself.

There are three ways in which you can use what you have just learned:

The first is as a way of answering questions and knotty problems. When you are immersed, take the time to ask yourself about a particular issue. A very useful tip is to see yourself reflected in the surface, and explain the problem very calmly and in detail. You can say it in your mind or aloud if you wish, the important point being to explain every aspect to yourself. Then imagine the tables are turned and allow your reflection to reply. It might ask more questions, ones you yourself had not even contemplated. It may suggest another person who can help. It could even give you the solution!

The second approach is not to ask any questions at all. Think back to your practice sessions—in particular to the time when you first felt immersed. I wonder if you somehow arrived at an answer to a problem that has been on your mind: the memory of an old friend you have lost contact with, perhaps, some important task, or simply where you had put your lost car keys! This is a great way to clear the mind of clouds and allow those lost memories to fly back home…

The third way involves you going much deeper and therefore takes a little more time. One very useful facet of this variation is that you can help other people with it by first guiding them into a relaxed state and then into a visualization. Rather oddly, I learned the original method for this at business school, but I have since adapted it to combine relaxation, visualization, and scrying.

GUIDED VISUALIZATION

**In many ways this final exercise sums up my philosophy of "fortune telling" quite neatly. The truth lies within you, and now you have some tools to help extract it.
I joined Amanda in a tranquil garden setting, to guide her on a journey of meditation, visualization and,
I hope, self realization.**

This method uses a script, although it is straightforward and rather self-explanatory, so it should not be difficult for you to learn. It does not matter if you make changes or leave parts of it out, just so long as the structure is there. Again, with this exercise you have two options: to have your querrant gaze into a reflective surface or to let them do it simply with their eyes closed. You can let the querrant or just circumstance decide which route you take. To prepare, sit your querrant in a quiet room or other tranquil place. Make sure they are comfortable and, most importantly, that they trust you. Let them choose something around them with which to scry: this might be a mirror, a candle, a bowl of water, or even a painting on the wall.

I brought Amanda to a peaceful garden to show you how this works. I do not need to know what may be bothering her or what questions she wants answers to: that is her business. And so the script begins. I spoke in a slow careful voice, making it rather monotonous, with little variation in the pace or volume:

Amanda, I want you to sit and relax. Place your arms at your side or on your lap, wherever feels most comfortable.
Close your eyes for me and take a deep breath in through your nose...

You might want to breathe along with them to show how.

…And out again very slowly through your mouth. Once again for me, in and out. One more time, in and out.

Now keep your eyes closed and let your mind wander. Do not "stare" but let yourself see a warm dull light in your mind. Let the light grow until it surrounds you. All you can see is that glow and what lies within it.

I want you to see yourself in the middle of the light. You are in a busy shopping mall. It is very brightly lit and there is a lot of noise, with many people bustling around and about. Can you see yourself there? Just nod if you can.

Good. Now walk over to the escalators and choose the one leading to the floor below. Feel yourself sinking slowly as it carries you further downward.

Feel the noise and crowds of the floor you just left rise above you as you descend to the next floor. It is quieter here; there are fewer people and not so much noise.

Head downward again on the escalator, toward another floor, which is quieter still and noticeably less bright. There is much less activity here; you feel calmer and more relaxed on this level—much more at home.

Go down two more floors, one at a time. With each successive floor, it seems calmer and more peaceful, as the hustle and bustle of the floors you have left behind float away above your head.

You are now on the first floor. There is little to see here other than a small desk which sits under a sign marked "HELP POINT." As you walk over to the desk, you are warmly greeted by a mature man with a kind face. He smiles and asks you to sit down and explain what you wish to know.

So, for the next few minutes, and in your mind only, tell him everything. You are on your own, so no one else can hear. Draw pictures to illustrate your story as you explain your situation to the man.

I paused for a moment, allowing Amanda to go over things in her mind, then continued:

The man smiles and thanks you for sharing your questions and concerns with him. He explains that he will consider your problem and will write to you shortly with the answer.

Now, Amanda, see yourself standing up and leaving the desk, thanking the man as you do so. Head for the up escalator and step onto it; feel yourself begin to climb slowly.

As you get to the next floor up, it becomes a little noisier around you. There is a small group of people here, who you pass as

you head further up and onto the next floor.

Continue feeling yourself floating upward and, as you go, you become more in touch with reality. Up one more level and you can see you are back in the shopping mall where you started a few minutes ago.

Let the light in your mind slowly shrink and fade away as you take three more breaths as before... Now open your eyes and stay relaxed.

Once they have undergone this experience, most people say they feel very relaxed and at peace. Amanda told me she felt "very calm" and "a little fuzzy." I asked her to sit for a while and her head was soon clear—clearer than it had been at the start! (I suggest you let your querrant relax for a few moments too.)

For some people, the answers to their questions will have already come. By asking your querrant to go over their issues carefully, calmly, and in a relaxed manner, they will often see solutions that were invisible to them beforehand, even if the answers themselves might be fairly straightforward! They may now understand what to do about a difficult relationship or where to find something they had mislaid—it is all dependent upon what they themselves asked.

Sometimes they do not have the answers straightaway, but, of course, the man did tell them that he would get back to them shortly. And, more often than not, at some point in the coming days a revelation or answer will pop into their head.

What we have done here is let our querrant's mind focus on an issue, to get it working on the problem in a subconscious manner. We have also let our querrant hand responsibility for the solution to the imaginary man.

A counselor or therapist would usually tell you that you must make your own decisions and find your own answers, albeit with a little help. This approach is entirely compatible with that philosophy, as it is the individual who finds the solution. The man is, in fact, a part of them—perhaps the older, wiser "parent" part of their whole being.

Thus, we have learned how to teach ourselves and help others to "see" with a greater sense of clarity. That for me is the greatest strength of a good fortune teller. Throughout the book I have touched on some of the moral issues and briefly described the context and settings for readings. Our next chapter deals with this most important aspect in greater detail.

A GOOD READ

HOW TO GIVE APPROPRIATE AND MEANINGFUL READINGS

You now have at your disposal a wonderful array of fortune-telling tools. Whichever set you choose to use, and even if you elect to seek out more from other sources, you are still only part of the way there.

By far the most important element of telling fortunes is finding a context, a setting in which to do it. There is also the vitally important question of ethics: it is crucial that you understand your role and what you can or should say, and what you most definitely should avoid discussing.

In this chapter we look at some of the lessons I have learned. Perhaps this will help you understand how to go about readings for yourself more easily.

READING TO UNDERSTAND

Like most teenagers, I was living in an "unknown country." The simple life I had wanted to enjoy in my formative years had been turned upside down by a mind–numbing cocktail of uncontrollable events and the heady rush of hormones racing around my body. I was beginning my journey into the real world!

In an effort to make some sense of it all, I would scan the daily newspapers seeking out my horoscopes. I began to get further confused. My parents got two daily papers and one evening edition, all of which featured an astrology column. After months of reading them, I came to realize that the advice given to us Leos was different in each paper. Not just in the fine detail but also in the overall meaning.

I recall one time reading something along the lines of "Today you feel you need to get out and enjoy life to the full" in one paper, and "Your common sense warns you to stay at home and renew your energies" in another. I pondered all day upon this dichotomy, only to be completely stumped by the evening paper which confidently told me, "This is a time of uncertainty. You do not seem to know what to do for the best."

I think that around this time I became more than a little disillusioned. If the astrologers were genuine, then how could there possibly be such a difference in their interpretations? Which version, if any, was the right one?

Not surprisingly, I started to turn to other methods of telling fortunes in an effort to clear my mind. I had already looked at the physical methods such as physiognomy and palmistry, but these were about other people. It was me and my future that I needed to know more about.

At this time, my interest in performing magic was growing, and so it was cards that I turned to. Then, when I was 13, I was given my first set of Tarot cards. I would play with these for hours, laying out spreads and seeing what the future held for me. I got further confused. Every reading that I did was different—there were conflicting messages coming from the cards.

For me, it was a break from fortune telling that helped me see the light. I did not intend to stop doing what I had enjoyed for so many years—it's just that at 18 years of age, with an income and a car, a young man has certain other priorities!

My interest in readings was rekindled whilst I was recuperating after an accident. My idle hands and busy mind engaged in fortune telling once more, although this time I had a much clearer vision.

I could see that by refocusing my attention and energies into understanding myself and others, I could gain a truer vision than if I attempted to see what fate had in store.

I therefore hope that the following guidelines will help you to give better and more directed readings and help you avoid some of the pitfalls. Most importantly, I hope you can use it to understand where the boundaries lie.

WHO ARE YOU?

This is perhaps the most important question you need to consider when embarking on "telling fortunes" or "giving readings." This is about your relationship with your querrant—the person you are offering to read.

Specifically, you must be very clear that, whilst there may be some skill and even art in fortune telling, it does not necessarily make you a better person than anyone else. With your readings you can offer insight and perhaps some vision, but be aware that this information is ultimately your opinion: it is by no means absolute and you should be careful not to present it as such.

You must also be particularly careful to

help your querrant understand the limits of the relationship. Some people can become addicted to having readings and they can become almost dependant upon their favorite fortune teller. If you see them reading too much into your opinion, your duty is to reset their expectations as gently as you possibly can. Constantly remind them that you are simply giving them another thread of knowledge that they can use in life. The other important thing to remind them is that ultimately they must make their own decisions, take care of themselves, and live by the consequences.

This leads me to another most essential set of guidelines.

WHO SHOULD YOU READ?

Perhaps this section should be called "Who Should You *Not* Read," for there are times in all our lives when we are more vulnerable and certainly more suggestible than others. A good fortune teller needs to be aware of whom he is reading. He or she needs to be aware of the whole person and of certain potential risk factors. The groups to be careful with are: children; those going through a bereavement or trauma; those with mental health or associated conditions; yourself.

Children

I recall my elder brothers and sisters talking about and playing with palmistry, astrology, and even ouija boards, when I was very small—perhaps as young as five or six years old. This certainly spurred my interest in the subject and, although my interest in conjuring came from another direction, I know that I would not be doing the job I love today if it were not for their influence.

Having said that, we must be particularly careful about giving readings for young children. Their ability to distinguish between reality and fantasy, coupled with their natural respect for adults, can result in them becoming distressed or confused about what they are being told.

A good way to introduce them to the subject, however, is to make a game of it: for example, give them a simple reading but keep it all within the context of what they are going to do that day. Imagine it is the summer holidays and you are trying to decide where to go today. Should it be the coast, the country, the zoo? Have a rune drawn and see what it suggests to you. As a family talk about where you think the rune is indicating you should spend your day. However, you should be responsible and careful not to give full, detailed readings to minors.

Those Experiencing Trauma

Sadly, we all experience times of loss, anxiety, and tragedy during our lives. Reading for someone who has just lost a loved one is a very sensitive area, yet it is a time when many seek the help of fortune tellers.

If you do a reading for someone at such a time, use it to help them see what they need to do to regain stability in their life. Remind them of important issues they may have overlooked such as resolving financial affairs and so on. Perhaps your reading can assist them in realizing that other people are there to assist—be it family, friends, or professionals. Whatever you see in your reading, it will imply that life does go on despite the pain they are currently going through.

I have strong spiritual beliefs. However, I would never imply that I had contact with their lost relative or friend. This can lead to false hope and perhaps a misplaced dependence.

I suggest you exercise extreme caution in this situation.

Those with Mental Health Issues

A much greater percentage of the population than we realize suffers in one way or another with mental health issues. Some have serious psychotic conditions, while others may simply be beset by varying levels of depression. As a result, some people may have a dependency on drink or drugs, or find themselves slipping into other forms of addictive or abusive behavior. The real challenge for you as a fortune teller is that more often than not, sufferers can hide these problems very well from the outside world.

If you know, or suspect, that your querrant may be suffering in such a way, then I suggest you avoid giving a reading if at all possible. You may do better to act as a good friend and listen and advise outside the context of fortune telling.

Yourself

The one person we have not mentioned so far is *you*. You can give yourself a reading, although it can be easy to "accidentally" overlook important issues. That is simple human nature.

Because of this, it may be more productive for you to allow other people to give readings for you—especially the personal and speculative ones—letting you focus on your inner self.

WHERE & WHEN SHOULD YOU TELL FORTUNES?

The choice of location and timing really comes down to the personal preferences of yourself and your querrant, but a basic rule of thumb is wherever and whenever you both feel at ease. This may be a simplistic answer, but it says it all—well, nearly all! There are other dimensions that you should consider.

Mood is extremely important. If you are tired, stressed, or "under the influence," a reading may not be appropriate. To give good readings for your friends you must be very firmly rooted in the now.

Your home or the home of your querrant are usually good places to give readings, unless,

for one reason or another, there are bad memories or negative emotions attached to those places. Of course, readings do not need to be given at home or even indoors. Any location that has good memories for you or that you find inspirational will make an excellent venue for readings.

Peace and calm are helpful. These enable you to get into the mood and let you focus more clearly. But the most important factor is confidentiality. You are about to embark on an open and frank discussion with your querrant—they must be sure that no unwanted person will hear what you both have to say.

WHAT METHOD OF READING SHOULD YOU USE?

The basic idea behind this book is to provide you with a complete set of fortune-telling tools. There are hundreds of different methods listed in the various books that I have studied—many of which are more than a little unusual, as you may have seen!

It is, of course, impossible to look at every single one of these methods in detail. You would need a book of this size to deal fully with any one of the subjects we have covered in the various chapters.

However, what I do hope you get from reading this book is a sense of the different classes of fortune-telling methods. My advice to you is to practice one of each class. You may not wish to use any of the methods I have written about here, and that is perfectly fine. It is more important that you feel at ease and can understand what you are working with.

A "personal fortune" method, such as palmistry or physiognomy, will assist you in understanding the nature of your querrant. This will give you a baseline from which you may begin.

A "speculative" method will enable you to explore possibilities, to toss things up into the air, and see if you can make sense of how they fall.

A "focused" method is concerned with true inspiration and inner knowledge. You know what is right and the answers are there to be found.

If you have sufficient time and energy, it is a good idea to try out a little of each of these with your querrant. If there is not time, then my advice is to choose the one that you feel is most appropriate for the particular situation. I'll let you decide!

CAN YOU READ IN GROUPS?

Yes, you can. Many people I know organize regular get–togethers where they enjoy each other's company, some refreshments, and a good conversation.

Sometimes they will give readings within the group with the marvelous advantage that there is a greater range of skills in the group than there would be in one individual.

If you decide that you would like to host your own "Fortune Telling Party" then do try to make sure that you have other activities for your guests to enjoy. A whole evening filled purely with readings can be a real drag. Play some games, have some good food, and enjoy the company!

Most importantly, keep it light. Avoid going down the route of creating a "dark" or overly mystical context for the evening. That may be perfect for Halloween, but it does not create a good environment for readings!

WEIRD &
WONDERFUL

THE MORE UNUSUAL SIDE OF FORTUNE TELLING

Have you ever tried to make sense of this world? No single concept has occupied more mental energy and philosophical verbiage than the question of "The Meaning Of Life." Our understanding of the world and life, at a practical level, has grown exponentially throughout history. Mankind has learned to observe nature at work and to correlate cause and effect to enable him to determine the rules by which he lives.

Man's ability to do this effectively has sometimes been hampered by a lack of scientific knowledge and a desire not to challenge authority. Thus, some of our assertions have been a little flawed. For example, let us say that you were robbed by a left-handed person at some point. Is it reasonable to assume that all left-handers are criminals? Of course not, but as a result of certain (often misplaced) assumptions, our ancestors certainly found some unusual ways of predicting the future.

In this chapter we will look at how some of the more obscure and interesting methods of fortune telling and pseudoscience are now used as a framework simply for having fun.

CEROMANCY

No single icon holds a more universal impor–tance to religious and spiritual practice than the humble candle. Since man first burned animal oils some 30,000 years ago, he has been enchanted and entranced by the wonderful gift of light.

During the Middle Ages, the precursors of our modern candles first appeared, and their use in religious ceremonies began to spread wildly. Seen as a symbol of life, inspiration, and indeed of God, it is no surprise that the ancient magicians and soothsay-ers saw their potential for use in their own rituals. No doubt they observed the strange yet wondrous shapes formed as the molten wax cooled, especially when dropped into water.

Thus, the art of ceromancy came into being: ancient fortune tellers would heat bowls of wax and pour or drip them into water to see what shapes they made. In a manner simi-lar to that used in tasseography (div-ination by patterns in tea leaves), they would interpret the shapes. For exam-ple, a bird might signify a journey or some forthcoming news, a heart shape might imply the love of another, and clouds could indicate troubles ahead.

When I was researching this book I came across an incorrect definition of ceromancy as a literal reading of the behavior of candle and its flame. This is, of course, a form of pyro-mancy—but there is no reason why the two cannot be combined!

If you are going to try ceromancy, it goes without saying that you should take very great care. You are dealing with a flame and very hot wax, and, whilst you may not burn yourself, it is still possible to drop wax onto your furniture and clothes.

One method is to choose a candle with a dark color (these are easier to see when in the water) and a plain bowl filled with water. Let the candle burn for a good time and perhaps watch the flame and see what that tells you. Then carefully tip the candle, letting the wax drip into the bowl. Who knows what shapes and meanings you will find?

PHRENOLOGY

Have you ever seen, perhaps at a flea market or thrift store, a white china bust with what looks like a map drawn on the scalp? This is a "phrenology bust" and it is used by a phrenologist to indicate the areas of the brain that process or control the different parts of our mind.

An 18th century Viennese doctor by the name of Franz Joseph Gall was the pioneer of this most unusual science, and his argument was this:

The brain is the organ of the mind. The mind is not a single thing but a collection of conscious and subconscious processes, each of which relate to a facet of human existence,

behavior, and nature. Any organ in the body responds to proper use by growing; muscles, for example, develop with exercise. Likewise, if a certain part of our body is well proportioned, we might have a tendency to excel at any activities employing that part. Thus, Gall argued that the various parts of our brain containing the components of our mind could be identified and measured, giving a way to determine an individual's characteristics and attributes.

And so he developed a system of feeling and recording the bumps on the heads of his patients, which gained great favor in the early 19th century. Like so many great theories, it was soon ridiculed and marginalized, though there are still practitioners around today, often giving readings for entertainment purposes.

In actual fact, Gall's theories were not that crazy at all, and the modern understanding of the way the mind and brain work together tend to support his concept, although it does seem that his map was (at least by modern day understanding) rather inaccurate. I am lucky enough to own a phrenology bust (pictured here). I will leave it to you to interpret your own head from the lines and contours drawn upon it.

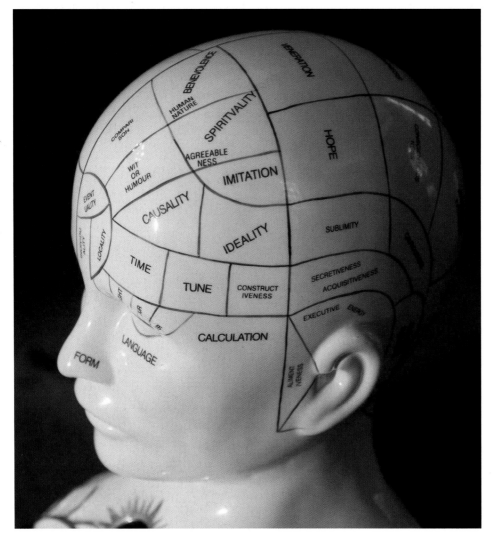

GEOMANCY

Geomancy is the name given to the use of forces from our Mother Earth for the purposes of prediction. This form of fortune telling has many faces in many cultures.

In the early 20th century, Alfred Watkins, a prominent British photographer, published a book which revealed a network of ancient pathways that stretched across the British Isles. He had begun to notice that churches, monuments, and other special places and structures all seemed to be located along discernible lines on the map. He called them "ley lines," and much research since then has shown further evidence of their existence.

Most of us are familiar with the concept of dowsing—using a stick or rods to find water. In fact, dowsers can also detect lines of energy and disruptions and anomalies. It is known that dowsers were used by ancient builders to help locate the best sites on which to construct churches. There are strong allusions to this even today in the mysterious rituals of freemasonry.

Feng Shui, which means "wind and water," is most popularly known as a technique for arranging your home and the rooms within it to obtain the best *Ch'i*, or energy. In fact, it is a far more complex science, sharing much in background and practice with dowsing, the lines in Feng Shui being known as *Lung-Mei* or "Dragon Lines."

These invisible forces can also be used to make predictions. Many cultures would scatter soil or small pebbles onto sacred ground and observe the patterns they made. Could it be that all the answers we need are within our Mother Earth, as well as within ourselves?

TASSEOGRAPHY

Tasseography is a rather elevated-sounding word for a rather stereotypical form of fortune telling: reading tea leaves.

You probably won't be surprised to learn that this practice began with the Chinese, who would drink their tea from cups that bore a close resemblance to the bells they used in their religious ceremonies. As a result, the tea cups took on a mystical significance.

The practice seems to have lost favor in recent years, most likely because we now drink our tea from mugs and use tea bags more often. Reading tea leaves is best done with a traditional china tea cup with a plain white inner surface. The tea should be made in a pot and poured, without using a strainer, and then drunk by the querrant. The querrant should leave a little tea in the cup and swirl it around three times, making sure the tea flows all over the inside surface. The cup should then be quickly laid down on the saucer while they count to seven.

The reader may then pick up the cup and hold it with the handle facing them, and the reading can begin.

There are two elements to consider in the reading: the shapes and images formed by the leaves, and the position of those images in the cup. The various books I have read on the subject generally deal with the relevance of each position. The upper area represents now, the middle and lower areas represent the future, and the bottom of the cup is associated with bad luck. The right-hand area represents the querrant, the middle the end of an influence, and the left a force coming into play.

However, the shapes are not so easy to specify. It is my recommendation that you see whatever image your own perception shows you and interpret that: shapes such as hearts might indicate love or care, birds might imply travel, and coins might imply money or wealth and so on.

CROMNIOMANCY

Have you ever heard the expression, "He knows his onions"? I have always been interested in the origins of words and phrases and I decided to research the source of this unusual phrase.

To my dismay I found out it had nothing to do with cromniomancy—the ancient art of fortune telling using onions. However, the humble onion has been important in both culinary and spiritual terms for many cultures for thousands of years.

It was a most holy vegetable to the ancient Egyptians, who believed its shape to be sacred. Onions appear frequently in Egyptian art, where there are many examples to be seen of men holding onions while they took important oaths. And, of course, the onion played a part in that most Egyptian of rituals, the embalming and mummification of the dead.

The Romans saw beauty and natural order in the concentric rings to be seen inside the onion: for them it represented the eternity of the universe. Indeed, onions have always been recognized for their antiseptic and purifying qualities: we all know that garlic (a close relative of the onion) can be used to ward off evil demons and vampires!

And so, it is no wonder that onions have taken on a spiritual meaning over the centuries and been used for divination from Europe to Asia.

The most common method of fortune telling using onions involves observing their sprouting behavior. Traditionally, a pair of onions might be inscribed with a "Yes" or "No," and left on an altar or special place while a question was asked. Whichever onion sprouted first would determine the answer.

In certain Germanic countries it has even become a tradition for young women to write the names of potential suitors on a number of onions: the one to sprout first would indicate their true love!

ORNITHOMANCY

Man has held no single creature in greater awe than the bird. Throughout history, he has been insanely jealous of our feathered friend's ability to fly, to go wherever it desires whenever it wishes. The bird symbolizes mankind's struggle to free himself from the shackles of his mundane day-to-day existence.

Birds had a special significance for the Greek and Roman civilizations, who both developed systems of divination, and indeed worship, using them.

Today we know that birds are aware of forthcoming changes in the weather and disturbances in the Earth's natural order. And, although scientists have yet to fully agree on exactly how birds navigate, we know that they do so using some form of heightened sense, perhaps magnetic, which tunes them in to their environment.

According to ancient records, the Greek philosopher Anaximander predicted an earthquake sometime in the 6th century BC by observing the behavior of birds. No one can be sure exactly what he saw, but we do know that birds will try to avoid or fly away from impending disasters.

The Romans developed a whole part of their religious system based on the study of birds. Priests called "augurs" would observe and interpret the behavior of all animals, and birds in particular. They watched flight patterns, interpreting movement from the right as good and the left as bad. They also paid attention to bird calls, with each call having a significance of its own. The more frequent or intense the call, the sooner or greater the impending event.

HIPPOMANCY

With the possible exception of the dog, man's greatest ally in the animal kingdom has to be the horse. He has used it to plow his fields, transport his goods, and carry his armies.

Horses appear frequently in mythology, sometimes carrying the gods across the night sky, and often auguring victory or acting as a portent for defeat or disaster.

Just think for a moment of the number of horses you know from ancient stories, such as Pegasus, the winged horse; the Centaur, half–man–half–horse, the Trojan horse; and the mysterious and magical unicorn. The horse is a noble and enigmatic creature, and one that seems to have great wisdom to impart to his master. As a result, man has found many ways to predict the future by observing and inter-preting their behavior.

Ancient Persian folklore tells us that kings would be chosen by horses. A group of victori-ous generals would mount their steeds at dawn and wait for the first neigh. Whichever horse made the first noise would determine the choice of new leader.

Medieval Germans kept their horses on holy ground in or around their churches. When, from time to time, they were preparing themselves to attack a foe or ride into battle, they would observe which of the horse's feet crossed the threshold first: the left foot was seen as a bad omen, and they would call the battle off.

BIBLIOMANCY

Ever since mankind developed the means to record his words on paper, a certain number of his writings have taken on special significance.

Every great religion, spiritual movement, and even the great secular societies have taken the words of their leaders, prophets, and thinkers, and held them in special regard, citing them to be "The Truth," "The Law" or "The Word of God."

So whether it be the Torah, Bible, Koran or even Mao's "Little Red Book" of quotations, there are great sources of considered thought, guidance, and advice available to anyone who needs them.

Some people take their inspiration from the intense study of these tomes—poring over every single word and phrase repeatedly, and committing them to memory. Others spend hours in intense debate with their peers, arguing over the precise meanings they contain.

Whatever book you decide to use for your inspiration, there is a method available that has been in use for millennia, which will enable you to receive advice immediately: this is the practice of bibliomancy.

The traditional method is to take your chosen book and stand it upright, resting on its spine. Close your eyes and let the book fall open at a random page. You then read the first passage or paragraph, and take whatever guidance or inspiration it offers you.

A more involved method requires you to keep your eyes closed and scan the pages with your hands, and, when you feel the moment is right, come to a stop. Read the words that are closest to your index finger and see what they have to offer.

There is one danger with this approach to seeking guidance: the book is most likely to

fall open at a page you have read frequently; perhaps this page contains your favorite words, so it would be no surprise if these were inspiring or comforting. Indeed, perhaps not understanding this physical characteristic of books led some early bibliomancers to read more into the art than they probably should have.

My suggested solution to this is to use a dice, cards, dominoes, or some other random device in order to select page numbers.

THE BOOK TEST

Not unrelated to bibliomancy is the idea of a the book test. However, despite the similarities, its purpose, concept, and origins are somewhat different.

In my research, I have been unable to find a definitive origin for the book test but it seems to have come about during the spiritual revival that started in the United States in the middle of the 19th century.

Rather than using the book as a form of random message divination (as in bibliomancy), the book test was derived to prove the existence of a departed spirit. Thus, during a séance, the medium would attempt to make contact with the departed relative of the querrant. They would be directed by the spirit to choose a book from a shelf, open it at a certain page, and read a particular passage.

This passage would supposedly have some relevance or importance to the querrant and act as "proof" that the medium was indeed communicating with a loved one "from the other side."

Of course, no matter what book, page, or passage was chosen, the medium would find some way of cleverly twisting the information to fit the relationship between the querrant and the departed spirit. If they couldn't make that work, their escape clause was to say it was an incomprehensible message from beyond!

Rather interestingly, the book test has been taken into the domain of performing mind readers or mentalists, who use various techniques to recreate the concept. In actual fact, it has now become a very standard plot, and justly so as it can produce great theater.

I have performed book tests for many years and have written about them in my previous books. There are many other odd methods of fortune telling that I have in the past adapted into magical performances, such as dermography and gyromancy, which follow.

DERMOGRAPHY

This is yet another ancient form of fortune telling that is widely used by magicians in an entertainment context.

In my book *Every Magic Secret in the World*, I describe a trick where the name of a chosen card appears on my forearm when I rub ash into my skin.

This relates to a practice that seems to have originated amongst Indian mystics. I have found a number of references to descriptions of this occurring, in much the same way as reports of the famous Indian Rope Trick.

The mystic would ask the querrant to consider some question of great importance to them and then write it out on a small piece of paper.

This note would be ceremoniously burned and its ashes gathered up by a "seer." The seer would rub the ashes onto a certain

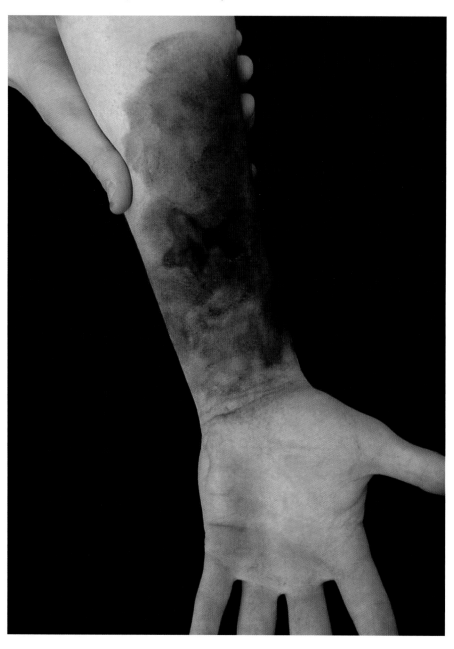

part of his body, such as his arm or even his fore-head. Markings or symbols would then mysteriously appear on his skin.

He would then proceed to "answer" the question that the querrant was considering, relating the symbols that had just appeared to what the quer-rant had asked of him.

Numerous mystics no doubt interpreted the vari-ous shapes and symbols in good faith, reading them in much the same way as you might tea leaves, look-ing for recognizable images in the shapes. On the other hand, many others proba-bly simply offered some generic answers, which seemed to make sense, while others no doubt used some form of trickery to find out what questions had been asked. In this way they could give apparently meaningful responses and appear to have truly mystical powers.

GYROMANCY

As the name implies, this is fortune telling by using circles, or by moving in or around circles.

Circles certainly do have strong mystical connotations. They represent wholeness and the never-ending cycles of life. They symbolize our Earth, our Sun, our hearts, and the eggs from which our life is born. You will, no doubt, already be aware they appear frequently in mystical symbolism.

There are a number of ways in which circles have been used for fortune telling and divination. One of these processes involves the fortune teller drawing a large circle on the ground, around which they would write the letters of the alphabet, or draw some mystical pictures or other symbols.

The fortune teller would then ask the querrant to walk continuously around the circle until they stumbled or even collapsed. The letter or symbol at which the querrant faltered would be interpreted to give some significance—for example, if they stopped on a particular letter that was an enemy's initial.

Another version from some African cultures involves an elder or "seer" spinning around in a circle, at an increasing speed, until they became so dizzy that they collapsed on the floor. In their intoxicated state, they would mumble incoherent ramblings, which would be noted and taken to be of great significance to the future of the village.

A simpler and far less energetic way of experimenting with gyromancy is to make a circle on a table top and lay letters, cards, runes, or other symbols around it, face downward and thus hidden. Your querrant may then count around the circle using a randomly chosen number, turning up the card at the position at which they came to a stop.

I adapted this idea for a magical routine in my book *Mind Magic*, but you could use it as a means of selecting a card or symbol from one of the speculative fortune-telling tools in this book.

GLOSSARY

With so many complex and ancient arts and sciences existing under the umbrella of fortune telling, it comes as no surprise that there are so many words, phrases, and names to remember and understand.

Many of these terms are fully explained elsewhere within the pages of this book. However, I have compiled this brief glossary of some of the important terms you will encounter (along with a few other words that you might come across) to help with your understanding.

Arcana—The plural of "arcanum," which describes ancient rituals and practices. Most commonly known used to describe the two sections of a set of Tarot cards.

Auras—The concept of lines of colored radiation emanating from the human body. Those able to see them interpret the auras in order to determine a person's character or detect health problems.

Biorhythms—A concept that implies that your physical, emotional, and intellectual energies ebb and flow through time in cycles of varying length. Thus, you should be mindful of where each energy level is in order to decide the best time to undertake a particular activity, for example.

Ch'i (Chi, Ki or Qi)—From ancient Chinese culture, the concept of *Ch'i* is of a positive life force that flows throughout the universe.

Clairvoyance—The ability to see in your mind's eye what may be happening in another time or place. Related to "clairaudience"—the ability to hear in a similar manner.

Conjure/Conjuring—Although this is a term that is commonally associated with stage magicians, the origins of the word are related to the ability to call up or create spirits and other mystical forces.

Crystallomancy—A method of fortune telling using crystals, either using them for scrying or by interpreting their behavior.

Divination—The ability to divine or find items or information using your own abilities. Closely related to "dowsing" and "psychometry."

Dowsing—The practice of finding water, metals, and other precious items using the forked branch of a tree, metal rods, a pendulum or other devices.

ESP (Extra Sensory Perception)—The ability to react to stimuli not associated with our normal five senses. It is often referred to as a "sixth sense."

Fate—The concept that our future or destiny has been predetermined, perhaps by some higher entity or deity.

Hydromancy—Fortune telling using water, by observing its color, its flows, or the movement of ripples, or perhaps by scrying.

Karma—An ancient Sanskrit word, which literally translates as "deed." A central concept in many Asian religions, it implies that we as individuals are the sum of all our actions past and present (both good or bad), and that this sets the course of what will happen to us. Put another way—"What goes around comes around"!

Medium—A medium is one who connects to the spirit world in order to tell fortunes or pass other information across. This is one of many terms that are sometimes incorrectly applied to anyone with "special abilities."

Nostradamus—Michel de Nostredame (1503–66) is perhaps history's best known "seer" and writer of prophecies. His writings—which were typically drug-induced—comprised a series of four line poems called quatrains. He is credited with foreseeing numerous historical events, from the rise of Hitler to the attacks of 9/11. However, his work is regarded by critics as too general—allowing for meanings to be broadly interpreted after an event.

Oneiromancy—Fortune telling through the interpretation of dreams.

Psychic—A general term used to describe special abilities, or anyone with those abilities that are related to an extra or "sixth" sense.

Psychometry—The concept that objects that we own, or even simply touch, absorb some of our energy. Thus, a sensitive person may be able to give information about an individual simply by touching an item of theirs, and never actually encountering them in person.

Pyromancy—Fortune telling using fire, by watching the movement of the flames, their color, or the patterns of the smoke.

Qabbalah (Kabbalah)—This is a doctrine of the Jewish faith, which concerns the true spirit of God, the earth, and nature. This esoteric knowledge has been handed down to only a select handful. Often incorrectly regarded as a threat to Christian doctrine, Qabbalah is some-times associated with secret societies such as freemasonry.

Querrant—The person for whom you are giving a reading, or whose fortune you are telling—more literally, the person who is questioning you!

Reading—A general name given to describe the act of or the product of a fortune telling session.

Seer—One with clairvoyant abilities.

Sitter—Another term which describes the person for whom you are reading—more correctly, one of those present at a séance.

Soothsayers—An ancient name for one who predicts the future for others. "Sooth" is an old word for "truth": thus, they can be called "truth tellers."

Soul—The ethereal substance that is the essence of any living thing. Many religions believe the soul to be immortal: for example, Buddhists believe that it may continually trans-fer to other living things, while Christians believe that it (hopefully) ascends to Heaven.

Spirit—Spirit is a very similar concept to "soul," although it has another connotation as a physical manifestation, such as a ghost or other presence.

Swami—A Hindu priest or yogi. One who has attained "mastery over himself" and thus may be considered pure, and is often considered to have the ability to see the future.

Séance—A meeting or ritual designed to make contact with those who have passed on to the other side. Typically led by a medium, who will let spirits enter the room through their own body: this is known as "channelling."

USEFUL ADDRESSES, WEBSITES & FURTHER READING

With so many different branches and so many different disciplines, your journey in the world of fortune telling may be very long and complex. To help you along your way I have listed some books, stores and other resources that will help you to find out more information and locate the tools you may need to explore some of the concepts covered in this book.

USEFUL ADDRESSES

The Astrological Association
Unit 168
Lee Valley Technopark
Tottenham Hale
London
N17 9LN
Tel: 020 8880 4848
Fax: 020 8880 4849
office@astrologicalassociation.com
www.astrologicalassociation.com

Plenty of useful information and links to international astrological resources.

The London Phrenology Company Limited
53 St Martins Lane
London
WC2N 4EA
Tel: 020 7836 0727
Fax: 020 7240 6697
info@london-phrenology.com
www.phrenology.co.uk

Probably the best starting point for phrenology on the web.

WEBSITES

www.lemezma.com
The author's own website.

www.geomancygroup.org
The website of the Geomancy Group, with useful information and links.

www.metta.org.uk
A holistic information service dedicated to complementary health and holistic information in the UK.

www.palmistry.com
A very useful multilingual palmistry website.

www.rune-stones.co.uk
A source of top quality runes.

www.somethingforthewickend.com
Candles, incense, and a large range of other products to help you set the mood.

www.thepsychicstore.com
A massive range of cards and other paraphernalia associated with the art of fortune telling.

BOOKS

The Book of Runes
Ralph Blum
(Connections)

The Palmistry Bible: The Definitive Guide to Hand Reading
Jane Struthers
(Godsfield Press)

Parkers' Astrology
Julia and Derek Parker
(Dorling Kindersley)

Personology: The Precision Approach to Charting Your Life, Career and Relationships
Gary Goldschneider
(Running Press)

The Tarot: History, Symbolism and Divination
Robert M. Place
(Jeremy P Tarcher)

Teach Yourself to Meditate: 10 Simple Exercises for Peace, Health and Clarity of Mind
Eric Harrison
(Ulysses Press)

Every Magic Secret in the World Revealed
Marc Lemezma
(New Holland)

Mind Magic
Marc Lemezma
(New Holland)

INDEX

Page numbers in **bold** indicate major references; those in *italics* indicate separate pages of illustrations.

ACKNOWLEDGMENTS

Of all the books I have written, this volume has been the most challenging. It represents a world which is at the very best nebulous and sometimes implicitly controversial.

Thus I am eternally grateful to the huge team of people who have helped me along the way: not least to Jo, Gareth, and Alan at New Holland for their undying support and confidence in me. I must also mention the whole New Holland team—some of whom have unwittingly found themselves part of this book!

My photographer Duncan Soar has done a most magnificent job, not least in making me look younger and even more debonair than I truly am... I must also thank Sue Mahor of Stone Castle (www.stonecastle.net) and Simon Lace and Kevin Brice from Maidstone Museum and Bentlif Art Gallery (www.museum.maidstone.gov.uk) for letting us use their magnificent facilities and for their generous co-operation.

Of course I must not forget my wife, Emma, who was there with the tea when I needed it, and my sons Dan and Josh for putting up with me continually asking them to keep quiet while Dad is writing!

I must also thank my "querrants" and models for their time and patience:

Joan Woodroffe, Gareth Jones, Gray Lappin, Cecilia Shakerley, Marion Storz, Gulen Shevki, Steffanie Brown, Kate Parker, Hema Gohil, Catherine Holmes, Adam Morris, Andrew Menniss, Sophie Legrand, Rupinder Virdi, Alan Marshall, Lauren Bennett, Ruth Hamilton, Hazel Kirkman, Charlotte Morgan, John Woolcott, Celia Pope, Alex Morris, Sue Maher, Lisa McGimpsey, Andrew Smith, Graeme Middleton, and Amanda Hawkins.

Finally, the biggest debt of gratitude is for those who have caused me to reflect on life and those "charlatans" who have inspired me to pursue a more honest path.

PHOTOGRAPHY ACKNOWLEDGMENTS

All photographs taken by Duncan Soar, apart from:

Pages 2 (right); 17–18; 70–73; 99 (top left); 113; 120—Alan Marshall

Page 116 (top)—David Tipling

Page 116 (bottom)—John Shaw/NHPA